ARTISAN BREAD MAKING

TABLE OF CONTENT

BREAD MAKING BASICS - TIPS AND TRICKS

Making your own bread is one of the most rewarding skills to master in the kitchen, and you don't need lots of gadgets or ingredients to do it! Bread making basics are a bowl, measuring spoons, a measuring jug and something to bake the loaf on or in – either a loaf tin or a baking tray. You could also try a baking stone, which you place in the oven increasing the bottom cooking temperature and meaning you can bake directly onto the hot stone; they are great for sourdoughs, flatbreads and pizzas.

For ingredients, you only need a good quality bread flour; yeast – cultured or naturally occurring as in a sourdough starter; water and sea salt.

Bread Making Basics - Which Bread Flour Should I Use?

Always use strong bread flour, either white or wholewheat. Stone-ground flour will give you better flavour, colour and texture. Bread flour has a higher gluten content than regular plain flour, which makes the dough stretchy and gives your finished loaf lightness and volume. You can make different types of bread with spelt and rye flours, which have lower gluten content and result in a denser loaf.

Bread Making Basics - Which Yeast Should I Use?

The ingredient that makes bread rise is yeast, and there are three types of yeast that you can use. Fresh yeast is available from bakeries and in-store bakeries in some supermarkets. It can be kept wrapped in the fridge for up to a week and for a month in the freezer. Fresh yeast isn't suitable for using in a bread making machine. You will need 25g fresh yeast for every kilo of bread flour. Dried active yeast comes in a tin and you mix this with warm water and a little sugar before combining with the flour, which means you can kick-start the yeast and check it is still alive (bubbles form on the surface of the water). Keep your open tin of dried active yeast in the fridge and use within three months. You will need two tablespoons of dried active yeast for 1 kilo bread flour. Finally, you could use sachets of fast acting yeast, which you add directly to the flour – they are easy to use and suitable for bread machines. You will need 2 x 7g sachets of fast acting yeast for every kilo of bread flour.

Bread Making Basics - Tip and Tricks

1. Cold doesn't kill yeast but excessive heat does, so don't add hot water to your yeast or leave dough to rise in a really hot place such as on top of an aga.

2. Kneading puts energy into the dough to stretch the gluten. The stretchier the dough, the better it will hold the gasses released by the fermentation of the yeast, and the better the texture of the bread. Knead for at least ten minutes.

3. The dough should be sticky, but not too wet, it should hold its shape and not flow over the work surface. When kneading start with a stickier rather than a drier dough as it will come together as you knead.

4. To check if your dough has been kneaded enough, lightly press with a finger the indentation should pop straight back, if it doesn't, knead more!

5. Cover your dough while it is rising to stop it drying out with cling-film greased with a little oil.

6. Most recipes recommend double proving your dough – this means leaving it to rise until doubled in size, then knocking it back to its original size, forming into shape or place in a greased tin and leave to rise again. By doing this you get a lighter, less yeasty, good textured loaf.

7. To improve the baking process preheat your oven to its maximum temperature and reduce to baking temperate when you put the loaf in, adding a spray of water from a simple (clean!) gardening spray creates steam, which promotes the baking process.

8. To test whether a loaf is cooked turn it over and tap the bottom, it should sound hollow. If not, pop it back in the oven for a few more minutes. It is a good idea to put the loaf back into the oven without its tin, or upside down if it's a rustic loaf to ensure that the base of the loaf is well cooked.

Bread Making Basics - Easy Recipes to Get You Started

Once you've mastered the basics the bread making world is your oyster. Here are a few of our favourite easy bread making recipes to get you started!

Rachel's Basic Bread Dough Recipe A basic bread dough recipe that works for everything - use it to make bread, pizza, rolls, pita bread, and flatbread.

Irish Soda Bread - Bread at its simplest, no yeast required!

Gluten Free Soda Bread with Linseed.

Pita Bread - plain or spiced up!

Lavash Bread - a simple unleavened flatbread

Focaccia Bread

French Fougasse - Beautifully shaped like the pattern on a leaf

BREAD BAKING FUNDAMENTAL TIPS

Man cannot live on bread alone. We have heard it countless of times in many variations depending on the religion in which the speaker is affiliated with. Regardless, it only shows that amongst all of vast variety of foods we have on the table, the bread represents all that is good in life. Or rather, it represents our very survival when our lives are stripped down to the basics.

It is indeed important to bake bread as best as you possibly can. After all, breads can form the basis of the entire meal from the appetizer (dip bread) to the main course (pizza) to desserts (cinnamon rolls). Well, here are tips and tricks to bake the perfect homemade bread.

Right Temperature

When preheating the oven, you must set the temperature at 50 degrees higher than the recommended baking temperature. As soon as the oven reaches the preheating temperature, place the bread dough inside, perform misting procedures and then lower the heat to the recommended baking temperature.

Keep in mind that breads can be baked anywhere from 350 degrees to 450 degrees. As such, you may also experiment with the heat until you get the desired results in terms of crustiness and tenderness of the bread. Take note that the emphasis is on experimentation when you have already acquired the necessary experience.

Right Shape

The beauty of breads often lies in their different shapes, with texture and taste coming in a very, very close second. Besides, the right shape of the bread dough affects how well it is cooked.

You will need to practice how to shape the bread dough especially as each one requires different techniques imposed either by tradition or by the type of dough. For example, Viennese bread has tapered ends while the French bread known as fougasse is flat and rectangular.

Right Misting

You must introduce humidity to the bread dough at the beginning of its baking cycle. This allows the bread to take on a golden brown, crunchy crust that makes for one of life's pleasures.

To achieve this effect, you should place an empty, clean pan into the shelf below the baking pan as the oven preheats. When you have placed the bread into the oven, pour a half cup of tap water into the preheated pan. This will introduce steam into the whole setup.

You also need to mist the top of the bread dough using a clean spray bottle. Immediately close the oven door after the misting but remember to do it again after 2-3 minutes for two more times. After that, leave the bread to bake to its full cycle.

HOT TIPS FOR MAKING PERFECT FRENCH BREAD IN YOUR OWN KITCHEN.

1. Go French and Don't Look Back. So what's so great about this whole "French-Technique" hoo-hah? It's all about the method of working (kneading) the dough which allows for a much looser, (wetter) mixture, that results in a lighter, springier, more elastic and responsive dough. This dough rises beautifully with no requirement for any improvers and produces a truly excellent texture of crumb and a light crispy crust, distinctive of French bread. These results are quite unlike those produced by other kneading techniques where recipes naturally demand a greater flour content to prevent the dough from sticking to everything as it's being kneaded. Breads produced in this manner will predictably be heavier, have a denser texture and a thicker crust.

2. Find a Baking Course. Understanding what it takes to produce superior bread is an experiential phenomenon. There's no other way to learn bake bread than to roll up your sleeves and get your hands in the dough. So first of all be ready to try and fail, and learn from your mistakes, that's the joy of learning, secondly find a baking course in your area where you can see for yourself just how to work dough and bake bread the traditional French way, get an understanding of all the techniques and a feel for how wet of sticky the dough should be Believe me it will be worth it.. A picture tells a thousand words but a demonstration tells a million.

3. Weigh ALL Your Ingredients. Especially weigh the water if you want to be able to repeat a result you must know exactly

what went to produce that result, measuring by volume just isn't accurate enough.

4. Take Notes. Always work to a recipe, but know that you will almost certainly need to make an adjustment. So make sure that you take notes of exactly what you've done, and then if you make an improvement you've got a new best recipe, and you know how to reproduce it. Knowing how to make adjustments is something that only experience will show you, but taking notes will speed this process along. If you don't take notes you're flying blind.

DIFFERENT TYPES OF BREAD AND THEIR BAKING TECHNIQUES

Bread is one of the first foods that humans began preparing for themselves eons ago. It is a staple for tons of meals and recipes, and knowing how to bake is an invaluable skill. Knowing how to bake bread is helpful when preparing all kinds of baked goods, including cookies, pastries, and cakes. This list of different kinds of bread will teach you about how many varieties of bread exist, and how they differ from one another.

Arepa – Arepa is a bread produced in South America. It has a similar texture to a soft tortilla, but is thicker, where tortillas are flat. It is made from maize flour, and frequently used for sandwiches with meat and cheese.

Baguette – Baguettes are a very popular type of French bread, characterized by their long tube-like shape, as well as their crunchy crust and soft interior. Baguettes can be up to two feet long, and are used for a variety of purposes outside of sandwiches.

BáhnMì – BáhnMì is like the Vietnamese version of a baguette. It is made with a combination of rice flour and wheat, and used almost exclusively for traditional Vietnamese sandwiches. Like a baguette, its crust is very crunchy while its inside is softer.

Bagel – Perhaps one of the most popularly consumed kinds of bread, bagels are made with yeast dough. They are rolled, boiled, and baked in an oven, and they have a denser texture than other types of bread. There are countless varieties and flavors of bagel available, including blueberry, everything, onion, whole wheat, and many more.

Bialy – A bialy is a round chewy roll, somewhat like a bagel, originally made in Bialystok, Poland. Bialys have a small indent in the center, which are commonly filled with onions and poppy seeds to provide flavor before they are baked. Like bagels, bialys are made with yeast, but they are prepared differently.

Breadstick – Breadsticks are available in nearly every restaurant in nearly every country of the world. They are long, thin pieces of bread that are baked for a long time, usually until they become crisp. The extra baking time lengthens the amount of time that the bread can be kept before being eaten.

Brioche – A brioche is a glazed roll with a sweet and rich flavor. It is often served with breakfast foods because of its sweetness. It is made by combining yeast with butter and eggs, and glazing with an egg wash after baking. Brioche is sometimes flavored, particularly with almonds.

Challah – Challah is a traditionally Jewish bread. It is braided before it is baked, giving it a very unique appearance. It has a sweet flavor, and is typically baked with yeast, eggs, honey, and flour.

Ciabatta – Ciabatta is an Italian loaf bread, with dense crumbs and a very hard and crisp crust. It is baked with wheat and often flavored with olive oil, rosemary or other spices, and dusted with flour when it comes out of the oven. Ciabatta is very frequently used for sandwiches, especially Panini, as it toasts particularly well,

Cornbread – Cornbread is made by baking corn that has been ground down into meal. Egg and buttermilk are often combined with the cornmeal before baking, making cornbread very cake-like in texture and taste. Cornbread can be very dense and crumby.

Croissant – Croissants are flaky, buttery, and very rich, and shaped like crescent moons. They are French rolls, made by baking puff pastry and yeast dough together in layers. Croissants are traditionally considered a breakfast pastry, and are often served with coffee in European countries, particularly France. Chocolate croissants are very popular as well; they are baked the same way, but a piece of dark chocolate is placed in the dough first.

Cracker – Crackers are like small segments of very crispy bread, originally made by combining flour, salt and water and baking the mixture. Crackers are distinguished from bread because they are not prepared with leavening. There are countless brands and flavors of crackers available today.

Crouton – A crouton is a small piece of very crunchy bread that has been baked twice, usually after bread has gone stale.

Croutons are cut into small cubes, seasoned, and used to garnish foods like soups and salads.

Date Nut – Date nut bread is made by combining dates, walnuts, and sometimes pecans, with egg, baking soda and a dough-like batter. It is rather rich and sweet, and is often topped with cream cheese.

Dough – Dough is used to make almost all bread. It is made by grinding grains down into a fine flour, and adding water. It is often seasoned, and leavening is added in order to allow the bread to rise when it is baked.

Dosa – Dosa is native to the southern regions of India. It is a very thin and flat bread, and is used to wrap fillings such as spiced vegetables and nuts.

English Muffin – The English muffin is a round yeast roll, often prepared by cooking dough on a griddle. Like a crumpet, an English muffin can be very dense and filled with air pockets. They are most often used as a breakfast roll, particularly as a base for breakfast sandwiches.

Focaccia – Focaccia bread was originally made in Italy. It tends to be relatively flat, as it is not kneaded before it is baked. It is not an entirely flat bread, because yeast is still one its ingredients, which causes it to rise slightly. Focaccia has a very rich flavor, and retains a lot of moisture, since it is brushed with olive oil before it is baked.

Fruit Bread – Fruit bread comes in almost countless varieties, consisting of dried fruit, and sometimes nuts. One of the most popular fruit breads is banana bread. Fruit bread is prepared very much like a cake, usually in a pan rather than as a freestanding loaf, and the mixture does not rise.

Hot Cross Bun – Hot cross buns are very sweet round rolls, made with yeast and raisins, and often with a cross shape cut into the dough before baking. They are frequently garnished with icing and served on the Christian holiday Good Friday.

Leavening – Leavening refers to the process by which bread is made to rise; this produces a lighter and chewier texture to bread. Leavening is accomplished by adding either chemical agents (such as baking powder or baking soda) or yeast to the dough prior to baking bread.

Marble Bread – Marble bread is made by combining pumpernickel and rye dough, and twisting the two together to create a swirl pattern in the finished product. Marble bread is baked in dense loaves and often used for deli sandwiches.

Matzo – Matzo is an unleavened flatbread, with a crisp and crunchy consistency similar to crackers, traditionally eaten on the Jewish holiday known as Passover.

M'smen – M'smen is traditionally made in Morocco. It is a flatbread, usually eaten as a breakfast food, with a flaky texture and a buttery flavor.

Naan – Naan is a Middle Eastern bread. It is a flatbread, similar to pita bread without a pocket. It is made by combining dough and leavening, and baking the mixture in a clay oven. Naan is sometimes served topped with butter, cheese, garlic, or spiced vegetables.

Panettone – A traditional Italian bread served at Christmas, panettone is prepared by curing dough for many days, then adding a variety of candied fruits, raisins, and sometimes lemon zest. The finished product is a tall loaf with an airy and light interior, and a sweet flavor.

Paratha – Paratha is an Indian flatbread similar to naan. It is prepared with whole wheat flour, which is then fried in oil. Paratha is frequently served stuff with cheese or vegetables.

Poori – Poori is another Indian bread made with whole wheat flour, combined with salt and water. The mixture is fried in oil, and the finished product looks like a puffy pillow.

Popover- A popover is a roll made by cooking egg batter in muffin tins. The rolls are crispy and light, with a hollow interior. Their name comes from the cooking method, which allows the batter to pop over the edge of the muffin cups.

Potato Bread – Potato bread was originally baked in Ireland, when a large amount of flour was replaced with mashed potatoes before baking bread. Potato bread has a denser texture than other breads, and a unique flavor.

Puff Pastry – Puff pastry is made by combining wheat dough with butter or fat, then rolling the mixture out many times over. Puff pastry is very flaky in texture and buttery in flavor.

Pretzel – Pretzels are made by rolling yeast bread into a long tube, and twisting and knotting the tube into a specific pretzel shape.

Pumpernickel – Pumpernickel bread is with a combination of sour dough and crushed rye grains, covered and baked at a low temperature for a long time. Pumpernickel can range from brown to black in color, and is frequently used to make deli sandwiches.

Rye – Rye bread is made from rye flour, which can range from light to dark based on the density and amount of fiber. Rye's flavor is much stronger than that of traditional wheat bread, and its texture is much more dense.

Scone – A scone is classified as a quick bread. They are prepared by combining flour, baking soda, sugar, eggs, milk and butter and baking the mixture. The texture of a scone is very dense and dry, with a very hard crust. They are traditionally eaten as a breakfast food, with butter, clotted cream, or honey, and are often flavored with fruit in the dough, such as blueberries or raisins.

Soda Bread – Soda bread is prepared by substituting baking soda for yeast in a traditional bread recipe. Soda bread is very sweet with a light texture, and is frequently flavored by adding nuts or raisins to the dough.

Sourdough – Sourdough bread is baked with certain bacteria that produce lactic acid and create a sour taste. Sourdough typically has a crispy outer crust and a softer, crumbier interior.

White bread – Classic white bread has actually been around for a relatively short time, compared to other breads. It is made with bleached, chemically refined white flour, resulting in its white color. Similarly, whole wheat bread is made with whole wheat flour, which is not refined.

BREAD RECIPES

Orange-Pecan Tea Bread

Ingredients

1 3/4 cups all-purpose flour

1 teaspoon baking powder

1/2 teaspoon baking soda

1/4 teaspoon salt

1/4 teaspoon ground nutmeg

1/4 teaspoon ground allspice

1/2 cup granulated sugar

1/2 cup low-fat buttermilk

1/4 cup chopped pecans, toasted

3 tablespoons 1% low-fat milk

3 tablespoons vegetable oil

3 tablespoons orange marmalade

2 teaspoons grated orange rind

2 large eggs

Cooking spray

1/2 cup powdered sugar

2 teaspoons fresh orange juice

1 1/2 teaspoons chopped pecans, toasted

How to Make It

Preheat oven to 350°.

Lightly spoon flour into dry measuring cups; level with a knife. Combine flour and the next 5 ingredients (flour through allspice) in a large bowl, stirring with a whisk; make a well in center of mixture. Combine granulated sugar and the next 7 ingredients (sugar through eggs), stirring with a whisk; add to flour mixture, stirring just until moist.

Spoon batter into an 8 x 4-inch loaf pan coated with cooking spray. Bake at 350° for 45 minutes or until a wooden pick inserted in center comes out clean. Cool 10 minutes in pan on a wire rack; remove from pan. Cool completely on a wire rack.

Combine powdered sugar and juice, stirring until smooth. Drizzle glaze over bread, and sprinkle with 1 1/2 teaspoons pecans.

Peanut Butter–Banana Bread

Ingredients

Bread:

1 1/2 cups mashed ripe banana

1/3 cup plain fat-free yogurt

1/3 cup creamy peanut butter

3 tablespoons butter, melted

2 large eggs

1/2 cup granulated sugar

1/2 cup packed brown sugar

6.75 ounces all-purpose flour (about 1 1/2 cups)

1/4 cup ground flaxseed

3/4 teaspoon baking soda

1/2 teaspoon salt

1/2 teaspoon ground cinnamon

1/8 teaspoon ground allspice

2 tablespoons chopped dry-roasted peanuts

Cooking spray

Glaze:

1/3 cup powdered sugar

1 tablespoon 1% low-fat milk

1 tablespoon creamy peanut butter

How to Make It

Preheat oven to 350°.

To prepare bread, combine first 5 ingredients in a large bowl; beat with a mixer at medium speed. Add granulated and brown sugars; beat until blended.

Weigh or lightly spoon flour into dry measuring cups; level with a knife. Combine flour and next 5 ingredients (through allspice) in a small bowl. Add flour mixture to banana mixture; beat just until blended. Stir in nuts. Pour batter into a 9 x 5-inch loaf pan coated with cooking spray. Bake at 350° for 1 hour and 5 minutes or until a wooden pick inserted in center comes out clean. Remove from oven; cool 10 minutes in pan on a wire rack. Remove bread from pan; cool.

To prepare glaze, combine powdered sugar, milk, and 1 tablespoon peanut butter in a small bowl, stirring with a whisk. Drizzle glaze over bread.

GRANDMA'S BACON AND CHEESE EASTER BREAD

INGREDIENTS:

8 cups all-purpose flour

2 cups whole milk

4½ teaspoons (2 packages) active dry yeast

2 tablespoons vegetable oil

2 tablespoons vegetable shortening, melted

6 eggs, lightly beaten

5 cups grated Romano cheese

3 (12-ounce) packages peppered bacon, cooked and crumbled

2 tablespoons butter, melted (for brushing the loaves)

DIRECTIONS:

1. Place the flour in a large mixing bowl; set aside.

2. Heat the milk in a small saucepan over low heat, stirring occasionally, until it is warm to the touch, but not hot. If you have an instant-read thermometer, the temperature of the milk should be between 110 and 115 degrees F. Once the milk reaches the correct temperature, remove from the heat, add the yeast, stir, and let sit for 10 minutes.

3. Add the milk and yeast mixture to the flour and begin to mix it into a dough (it will be shaggy at this point). Next, add the vegetable oil and melted shortening and continue to mix. Now, add the eggs and continue mixing until the dough forms a rough ball.

4. Turn the dough out onto a floured surface and knead it, adding more flour as necessary, until it is smooth and elastic,

about 5 minutes. Divide the dough into two and cover one half with a dish towel while you work with the other.

5. Working with one piece of dough at a time, roll it out very thin, into a large rectangle about 12x24-inches. Sprinkle the dough with half of the cheese, and then with half of the bacon, leaving a half inch border around all of the edges.

6. Starting with a long end facing you, roll the dough up into a tight cylinder jelly roll-style, pinching the seams and ends to seal. Once you have finished rolling the dough, gently coil it into a spiral into a pie plate. Repeat with the second piece of dough.

7. Once both loaves have been shaped and placed into pie plates, brush them with melted butter and then cover loosely with plastic wrap. Place in a draft-free area and allow to rise until almost doubled in size, 1 to 2 hours, depending on the temperature and humidity.

8. Preheat the oven to 350 degrees F. Bake the bread until golden brown on top, about 35 to 40 minutes. Allow to cool to warm room temperature before slicing them (ideally, let them cool completely, but sometimes I just can't wait!). Leftovers should be wrapped in plastic wrap and can be kept at room temperature for up to 5 days. The bread can also be frozen - be sure sure to wrap it tightly in plastic wrap, and then in aluminum foil.

APRICOT CREAM CHEESE BABKA

INGREDIENTS:

For the Dough:

1¾ cups + 2 tablespoons all-purpose flour

2 tablespoons + 1 teaspoon granulated sugar

1 teaspoon instant yeast

Pinch of salt

1 egg, at room temperature

⅓ cup whole milk, lukewarm

½ teaspoon vanilla extract

2 tablespoons unsalted butter, at room temperature

For the Apricot Filling:

1½ cups dried apricots

½ cup orange juice

⅓ cup lemon juice

2 tablespoons granulated sugar

For the Cream Cheese Filling:

8 ounces cream cheese, at room temperature

2 tablespoons granulated sugar

1 egg yolk

1 teaspoon vanilla extract

Pinch of salt

For the Streusel:

¾ cup all-purpose flour

2 tablespoons granulated sugar

4½ teaspoons light brown sugar

Pinch of salt

3½ tablespoons unsalted butter, melted and cooled

For the Egg Wash:

1 egg

Pinch of salt

DIRECTIONS:

1. Make the Dough: Place the flour, sugar, yeast and salt in the bowl of an electric mixer fitted with a dough hook. Stir on medium-low speed for a minute or so to combine. Add the egg, milk, vanilla and butter and mix on medium speed until a smooth dough forms, about 5 minutes. Form into a ball and place in a lightly oiled bowl. Cover with plastic wrap and place in a draft-free area until doubled in volume (about 1 hour). While the dough rests, make the fillings and streusel.

2. Make the Apricot Filling: Combine the dried apricots, orange juice, lemon juice and sugar in a small saucepan and bring to a simmer over medium-low heat. Simmer uncovered for 10 to 15 minutes, stirring occasionally, until the apricots soften and the liquid is reduced by half. Remove from the heat and allow to cool completely. Once cool, transfer the mixture to a food processor and process until a puree forms. Set aside at room temperature.

3. Make the Cream Cheese Filling: In a medium bowl, stir the cream cheese and sugar with a wooden spoon until smooth and lump-free. Add the egg yolk, vanilla extract and salt, and stir to combine. Set aside at room temperature.

4. Make the Streusel: In a medium bowl, whisk together the flour, sugars and salt. Add the butter and mix with a rubber spatula until the mixture comes together into large, coarse crumbs. Cover and refrigerate until ready to use.

5. Assemble the Babka: Lightly grease a 9×5-inch loaf pan; set aside.

6. On a lightly floured surface, roll the dough out into a 10×24-inch rectangle, with the long edge facing you. Spread the apricot filling evenly over the dough, leaving a ½-inch border along all of the edges. Spread the cream cheese filling over the apricot filling.

7. Starting with the bottom edge, roll the dough into the middle of the rectangle, then do the same with the top edge so that the two rolls meet in the center. Visualize the long cylinder divided into three equal lengths. Fold the left third over onto the middle third. Then, fold the right third over the middle third. Pick up the dough and turn it over so the seam is on the bottom. Then, holding each end, gently twist it in the middle and place it in the prepared pan.

8. Whisk together the egg and salt for the egg wash and brush it over the babka. Lightly cover the pan with plastic wrap and

place it in a draft-free area until it is doubled in size, 1½ to 2 hours.

9. Preheat oven to 375 degrees F. Brush the babka once again with the egg wash and sprinkle the streusel evenly over the top, pressing lightly so the crumbs adhere to the babka. Bake until the top is a deep golden brown, about 50 minutes. Cool the bread in the pan set on a wire rack for 25 minutes, then unmold the bread from the pan (some of the streusel may fall off) and place on the wire rack to cool completely. The bread will keep, wrapped tightly in plastic wrap, for up to 3 days.

AMERICAN SANDWICH BREAD

INGREDIENTS:

3¾ cups (18¾ ounces) unbleached all-purpose flour, plus more for dusting the work surface

2 teaspoons salt

1 cup warm whole milk (about 110 degrees)

1/3 cup warm water (about 110 degrees)

2 tablespoons unsalted butter, melted

3 tablespoons honey

1 envelope (about 2¼ teaspoons) instant yeast

DIRECTIONS:

1. Adjust an oven rack to the lowest position and heat the oven to 200 degrees. Once the oven temperature reaches 200 degrees, maintain the heat for 10 minutes, then turn off the oven.

2. Mix 3½ cups of the flour and the salt in the bowl of a standing mixer fitted with the dough hook. Mix the milk, water, butter, honey, and yeast in a 4-cup liquid measuring cup. Turn the machine to low and slowly add the liquid. When the dough comes together, increase the speed to medium and mix until the dough is smooth and satiny, stopping the machine two or three times to scrape dough from hook, if necessary, about 10 minutes. (After 5 minutes of kneading, if the dough is still sticking to the sides of the bowl, add flour, 1 tablespoon at a time and up to ¼ cup total, until the dough is no longer sticky.) Turn the dough onto a lightly floured work surface; knead to form a smooth, round ball, about 15 seconds.

3. Place the dough in a very lightly oiled large bowl, rubbing the dough around the bowl to coat lightly. Cover the bowl with plastic wrap and place in the warmed oven until the dough doubles in size, 40 to 50 minutes.

4. Gently press the dough into a rectangle 1 inch thick and no longer than 9 inches. WIth a long side facing you, roll the dough firmly into a cylinder, pressing with your fingers to make sure the dough sticks to itself. Turn the dough seam-side up and pinch it closed. Place the dough seam-side down in a greased 9 by 5-inch loaf pan and press it gently so it touches all four sides of the pan. Cover with plastic wrap; set aside in a warm spot until the dough almost doubles in size, 20 to 30 minutes.

5. Keep one oven rack at the lowest position and place the other at the middle position and heat the oven to 350 degrees. Place an empty baking pan on the bottom rack. Bring 2 cups of water to a boil in a small saucepan. Pour the boiling water into the empty pan on the bottom rack at set the loaf onto the middle rack. Bake until an instant-read thermometer inserted at an angle from the short end just above the pan rim into the center of the loaf read 195 degrees, 40 to 50 minutes. Remove the bread from the pan, transfer to a wire rack, and cool to room temperature. Slice and serve.

BAGELS

INGREDIENTS:

Sponge

1 teaspoon (.11 ounce) instant yeast

4 cups (18 ounces) unbleached high-gluten or bread flour

2 ½ cups (20 ounces) water, at room temperature

Dough

½ teaspoon (.055 ounces) instant yeast

3 ¾ cups (17 ounces) unbleached high-gluten or bread flour

2 ¾ teaspoons (.7 ounce) salt

2 teaspoons (.33 ounce) malt powder OR 1 tablespoon (.5 ounce) dark or light malt syrup, honey, or brown sugar

To Finish

1 tablespoon baking soda

Cornmeal or semolina flour for dusting

Sesame seeds, poppy seeds, kosher salt, rehydrated dried minced garlic or onions, or chopped fresh onions that have been tossed in oil (optional)

DIRECTIONS:

1. To make the sponge, stir the yeast into the flour in a 4-quart mixing bowl. Add the water, whisking or stirring only until it forms a smooth, sticky batter (like pancake batter). Cover the bowl with plastic wrap and leave at room temperature for approximately 2 hours, or until the mixture becomes very foamy and bubbly. It should swell to nearly double in size and collapse when the bowl is tapped on the countertop.

2. To make the dough, in the same mixing bowl (or in the bowl of an electric mixer), add the additional yeast to the sponge and stir. Then add 3 cups of the flour and all of the salt and malt. Stir (or mix on low speeds with the dough hook) until the ingredients form a ball, slowly working in the remaining ¾ cup flour to stiffen the dough.

3. Transfer the dough to the counter and knead for at least 10 minutes (or for 6 minutes by machine). The dough should be firm, stiffer than French bread dough, but still pliable and smooth. There should be no raw flour - all the ingredients should be hydrated. The dough should pass the windowpane test and register 77 to 81 degrees F. If the dough seems dry and rips, add a few drops of water and continue kneading. If the dough seems tacky or sticky, add more flour to achiever the stiffness required. The kneaded dough should feels satiny and pliable but not be tacky.

4. Immediately divide the dough into 4 ½ ounce pieces for standard bagels, or smaller if desired. Form the pieces into rolls.

5. Cover the rolls with a damp towel and allow them to rest for approximately 20 minutes.

6. Line 2 sheet pans with baking parchment and mist lightly with spray oil. Proceed with shaping the bagels.

7. Place each of the shaped pieces 2 inches apart on the pan. Mist the bagels very lightly with the spray oil and slip each pan into a food-grade plastic bag, or cover loosely with plastic wrap. Let the pans sit at room temperature for about 20 minutes.

8. Check to see if the bagels are ready to be retarded in the refrigerator by using the "float test". Fill a small bowl with cool or room-temperature water. The bagels are ready to be retarded when they float within 10 seconds of being dropped into the water. Take one bagel and test it. if it floats, immediately return the tester bagel to the pan, pat it dry, cover the pan, and place it

in the refrigerator overnight (it can stay in the refrigerator for up to 2 days). If the bagel does not float, return it to the pan and continue to proof the dough at room temperature, checking back every 10 to 20 minutes or so until a tester floats. The time needed to accomplish the float will vary, depending on the ambient temperature and the stiffness of the dough.

9. The following day (or when you are ready to bake the bagels), preheat the oven to 500 degrees F with the two racks set in the middle of the oven. Bring a large pot of water to a boil (the wider the pot the better), and add the baking soda. Have a slotted spoon or skimmer nearby.

10. Remove the bagels from the refrigerator and gently drop them into the water, boiling only as many comfortably fit (they should float within 10 seconds). After 1 minute flip them over and boil another minute. If you like very chewy bagels, you can extend the boiling to 2 minutes per side. While the bagels are boiling, sprinkle the same parchment-line sheet pans with cornmeal or semolina flour. (If you decided to replace the paper, be sure to spray the new paper lightly with spray oil to prevent the bagels from sticking to the surface.) If you want to top the bagels, do so as soon as they come out of the water. You can use any of the suggestions in the ingredients list or a combination. I make a seed and salt blend.

11. When all the bagels have been boiled, place the pans on the 2 middle shelves in the oven. Bake for approximately 5 minutes, then rotate the pans, switching shelves and giving the pans a 180-degree rotation. (If you are baking only 1 pan, keep it on the center shelf but still rotate 180 degrees.) After the rotation, lower the oven setting to 450 degrees F and continue baking for about 5 minutes, or until the bagels turn light golden brown. You may bake them darker if you prefer.

12. Remove the pans from the oven and let the bagels cool on a rack for 15 minutes or longer before serving.

CHOCOLATE BABKAS

INGREDIENTS:

1½ cups warm milk (110°F)

2 envelopes (¼ ounce each) active dry yeast

1¾ cups plus a pinch of sugar

3 whole large eggs, plus 2 large egg yolks, room temperature

6 cups all-purpose flour, plus more for dusting

1 teaspoon salt

3½ sticks (1¾ cups) unsalted butter, cut into 1-inch pieces, room temperature, plus more for bowl and pans

2 pounds semisweet chocolate, very finely chopped

1 tablespoon plus 1 teaspoon ground cinnamon

1 tablespoon heavy cream

For Streusel Topping:

1-2/3 cups confectioners' sugar

1-1/3 cups all-purpose flour

1½ sticks (¾ cup) unsalted butter, room temperature

DIRECTIONS:

1. In a small bowl, sprinkle yeast and a pinch of sugar over the warm milk; stir until dissolved. Let stand until foamy, about 5 minutes. In a medium bowl, whisk together ¾ cup sugar, 2 eggs, and the yolks; add yeast mixture, and whisk to continue.

2. In the bowl of an electric mixer fitted with the paddle attachment, combine flour and salt. Add the egg mixture, and

beat on low speed until almost all the flour is incorporated, about 30 seconds. Switch to the dough hook. Add 2 sticks butter, and beat until completely incorporated and a smooth, soft dough forms, about 10 minutes. The dough should still be slightly sticky when squeezed

3. Turn out dough onto a lightly floured work surface, and knead a few times until smooth. Place dough in a well-buttered bowl, and turn to coat with butter. Cover tightly with plastic wrap. Let rise in a warm place until doubled in bulk, about 1 hour.

4. To make the Streusel Topping:Combine sugar and flour in a large bowl. Using a pastry blender, cut in butter until mixture resembles coarse crumbs with some larger clumps remaining. Set aside.

5. In a bowl, stir together chocolate, remaining cup sugar, and the cinnamon. Using a pastry blender, cut in remaining 1½ sticks butter until combined; set aside filling.

6. Generously butter three 9-by-5-by-2¾-inch loaf pans and line with parchment paper, leaving a 1½-inch overhang along the sides. Brush more butter over the parchment, and set aside. Punch down the dough, and transfer to a clean work surface. Let the dough rest 5 minutes.

7. Meanwhile, beat the remaining egg with the cream. Cut dough into three equal pieces. On a well-floured work surface, roll out one piece of dough to a 16-inch square, about 1/8 inch thick. (Keep other pieces covered with plastic wrap while you work.) Brush edges of dough with the egg wash. Crumble one-third of the chocolate filling evenly over dough, leaving about a ½-inch border on the long sides. Roll up dough lengthwise into a tight log, pinching ends together to seal. Twist dough evenly down the length of the log, a full five or six times. Brush the top of the log with egg wash. Crumble 2 tablespoons filling down the center of the log, being careful not to let mixture slide off. Fold log in half into a horseshoe shape, then cross the right half over the left.

Pinch ends together to seal and form a figure eight. Twist two more times, and fit into a prepared pan. Repeat with remaining dough and filling.

8. Preheat the oven to 350°F, with a rack in the lower third. Brush the top of each loaf with egg wash; sprinkle with one-third of the Streusel Topping. Loosely cover each pan with plastic wrap, and let rise in a warm place until dough has expanded and feels pillowy, about 40 minutes.

9. Bake loaves, rotating halfway through, until golden, about 55 minutes. Reduce oven temperature to 325°F; bake until loaves are deep golden, 20 to 30 minutes more. (If the tops begin to brown too quickly, tent with aluminum foil.) Transfer pans to wire racks to cool completely. Babkas can be wrapped in plastic and kept at room temperature for up to 3 days.

CIABATTA BREAD

INGREDIENTS:

For the Sponge:

1 cup all-purpose flour

⅛ teaspoon instant (rapid-rise) yeast

½ cup water, at room temperature

For the Dough:

2 cups all-purpose flour

1½ teaspoons salt

½ teaspoon instant (rapid-rise) yeast

¾ cup water, at room temperature

¼ cup whole or 2% milk, at room temperature

DIRECTIONS:

1. Make the Sponge: Combine the flour, yeast and water in a medium bowl and stir with a wooden spoon until a uniform mass forms. Cover the bowl tightly with plastic wrap and let stand at room temperature for at least 8 hours or up to 24 hours.

2. Make the Dough: Place the sponge and the dough ingredients (flour, salt, yeast, water and milk) in the bowl of a stand mixer fitted with the paddle attachment. Mix on low speed until combined and a shaggy dough forms, about 1 minute, scraping down the bowl and paddle as needed. Increase the speed to medium-low and continue mixing until the dough becomes a uniform mass that collects on the paddle and pulls away from the sides of the bowl, 4 to 6 minutes.

Change to the dough hook and knead the bread on medium speed until smooth and shiny (the dough will be very sticky), about 10 minutes.

Transfer the dough to a large bowl, cover tightly with plastic wrap, and let rise at room temperature until doubled in size, about 1 hour.

3. Spray a rubber spatula or bowl scraper with non-stick cooking spray. Fold the dough over itself by gently lifting and folding the edge of the dough toward the middle. Turn the bowl 90 degrees, and fold again. Turn the bowl and fold the dough 6 more times (for a total of 8 times).

Cover with plastic wrap and let rise for 30 minutes.

4. Repeat the folding as in step #3, replace the plastic wrap, and let rise until doubled in size, about 30 minutes.

5. One hour before baking, adjust an oven rack to the lower-middle position, place a baking stone on the rack and preheat the oven to 450 degrees F.

6. Cut two 12×6-inch pieces of parchment paper and dust liberally with flour. Transfer the dough to a floured work surface, being careful not to deflate it completely. Liberally flour the top of the dough and divide it in half with a bench scraper. Turn 1 piece of dough cut-side-up and dust with flour. With well-floured hands, press the dough into a rough 12×6-inch rectangle. Fold the shorter sides of the dough toward center, overlapping them like you would fold a letter in thirds, to form a 7×4-inch rectangle. Repeat with the second piece of dough.

7. Gently transfer each loaf, seam-side-down, to the parchment sheets, dust with flour, and cover with plastic wrap. Let the loaves sit at room temperature for 30 minutes (the surface of the loaves will develop small bubbles).

8. Slide the parchment pieces with the loaves onto a pizza peel. Using floured fingertips, evenly poke the entire surface of each loaf to form a 10×6-inch rectangle; spray the loaves lightly with water. Slides the loaves and parchment onto the baking stone. Bake, spraying the loaves with water twice more during the first 5 minutes of baking time, until the crust is deep golden brown and the loaves register 210 degrees F, 22 to 27 minutes.

9. Transfer the loaves to a wire rack, discard the parchment, and let cool to room temperature for at least 1 hour before slicing and serving. The bread can be wrapped in a double layer of plastic wrap and stored at room temperature for up to 3 days. Wrapped with an additional layer of foil, the bread can be frozen for up to 1 month. To recrisp the crust, thaw the bread at room temperature (if frozen), and place unwrapped bread in 450-degree oven for 6 to 8 minutes.

PANETTONE [ITALIAN CHRISTMAS BREAD]

INGREDIENTS:

1 cup raisins

2 tablespoons light rum

2 tablespoons hot water

3¾ cups all-purpose flour

⅔ cup granulated sugar

½ teaspoon active dry yeast

½ teaspoon salt

¼ teaspoon lemon zest

½ vanilla bean, split in half lengthwise

3 eggs, at room temperature

⅔ cup tepid water

1 tablespoon honey

10½ tablespoons unsalted butter, well softened

1 tablespoon unsalted butter, melted

1 tablespoon unsalted butter, chilled

⅔ cup candied citron (I used candied orange peel) in ¼-inch pieces

DIRECTIONS:

In a small bowl, combine the raisins with the rum and 2 tablespoons of hot water. Allow to soak at room temperature, stirring occasionally, until the raisins are plump and most of the liquid has been absorbed, at least 8 hours or overnight.

In a stand mixer fitted with a paddle attachment, mix together the flour, sugar, yeast, salt, lemon zest and vanilla bean on low speed until combined. In a medium bowl, whisk together the eggs, tepid water and honey. With the mixer on low speed, pour the egg mixture into the flour mixture. Increase the speed to medium-low and mix until all of the ingredients are combined. Add the softened butter, 1 tablespoon at a time, mixing until incorporated before adding more. Increase the speed to medium-high and beat until the dough is smooth and elastic, about 8 minutes.

Drain the raisins, discard the soaking liquid, and stir together with the candied citron and 1 tablespoon of melted butter. Stir this mixture into the dough with a wooden spoon.

Place the dough in a large bowl, cover with plastic wrap, and let rise in a cold oven with the door closed until it has nearly tripled in volume, 12 to 15 hours.

Locate and discard the vanilla bean, then sprinkle the dough lightly with flour and scrape out onto a lightly floured surface. Sprinkle a bit more flour onto the dough, then fold the edges of the dough in towards the center, forming a loose ball, and place, seam-side down, into the panettone mold. Cover with a damp kitchen towel (not terry cloth) and let rise in a draft-free place at warm room temperature until the dough is just above the top of the mold, 3 to 5 hours.

Preheat oven to 370 degrees F.

Place the dough-filled panettone mold on a baking sheet. Use a very sharp serrated knife to score an "X" across the entire surface of the dough. Place the 1 tablespoon chilled butter in the center of the X and bake until a wooden skewer inserted into the center comes out slightly moist but not wet, 60 to 75 minutes (the panettone will be very dark).

Remove from the oven and pierce 12-inch metal or wooden skewers all the way through the panettone (including the paper) 4 inches apart and 1 inch from the bottom so the skewers are parallel. Hang the panettone upside down over a large stockpot and cool completely before cutting. To store the panettone, wrap tightly in plastic wrap, then either place in a resealable plastic bag, or wrap again in foil. The bread will keep at room temperature for up to 1 week.

MONKEY BREAD

INGREDIENTS:

Dough:

4 tablespoons unsalted butter, divided, 2 tablespoons softened and 2 tablespoons melted

1 cup milk, warm (about 110 degrees F)

1/3 cup water, warm (about 110 degrees F)

¼ cup granulated sugar

1 package instant yeast

3¼ cups all-purpose flour, plus extra for work surface

2 teaspoons salt

Brown Sugar Coating:

1 cup light brown sugar

2 teaspoons ground cinnamon

8 tablespoons unsalted butter (1 stick), melted

Glaze:

1 cup confectioners' sugar

2 tablespoons milk

DIRECTIONS:

1. Butter Bundt pan with 2 tablespoons softened butter. Set aside.

2. In a large measuring cup, mix together milk, water, melted butter, sugar and yeast. Mix flour and salt in standing mixer fitted with dough hook. Turn machine to low and slowly add

milk mixture. After dough comes together, increase speed to medium and mix until dough is shiny and smooth, 6 to 7 minutes. Turn dough onto lightly floured counter and knead briefly to form smooth, round ball. Coat large bowl with nonstick cooking spray. Place dough in bowl and coat surface of dough with cooking spray. Cover bowl with plastic wrap and place in a draft-free area until dough doubles in size, 50 to 60 minutes.

3. For the sugar coating: While the dough is rising, mix brown sugar and cinnamon together in a bowl. Place melted butter in second bowl. Set aside.

4. To form the bread: Gently remove the dough from the bowl, and pat into a rough 8-inch square. Using a bench scraper or knife, cut dough into 64 pieces.

5. Roll each dough piece into a ball. Working one at a time, dip the balls into the melted butter, allowing excess butter to drip back into the bowl. Roll in the brown sugar mixture, then layer balls in the Bundt pan, staggering seams where dough balls meet as you build layers.

6. Cover the Bundt pan tightly with plastic wrap and place in draft-free area until dough balls are puffy and have risen 1 to 2 inches from top of pan, 50 to 70 minutes.

7. Preheat oven to 350 degrees F. Unwrap the pan and bake until the top is deep brown and caramel begins to bubble around the edges, 30 to 35 minutes. Cool in the pan for 5 minutes, then turn out onto a platter and allow to cool slightly, about 10 minutes.

8. For the glaze: While the bread cools, whisk the confectioners' sugar and milk in a small bowl until the lumps are gone. Using a whisk, drizzle the glaze over the monkey bread, letting it run over top and down the sides of the bread. Serve warm.

*Note: To make without a stand mixer: In step 2, mix the flour and salt in a large bowl. Make a well in the flour, then add the milk mixture to the well. Using a wooden spoon, stir until the dough becomes shaggy and is difficult to stir. Turn out the dough onto a lightly floured work surface and begin to knead, incorporating the shaggy scraps back into the dough. Knead until dough is smooth and satiny, about 10 minutes. Shape into a taut ball and proceed as directed.

CINNAMON SUGAR PULL-APART BREAD

INGREDIENTS:

For the Dough:

2¾ cups plus 2 tablespoons all-purpose flour, divided

¼ cup granulated sugar

2¼ teaspoons (1 envelope) active dry yeast

½ teaspoon salt

2 ounces unsalted butter

1/3 cup whole milk

¼ cup water

2 eggs, at room temperature

1 teaspoon pure vanilla extract

For the Filling:

1 cup granulated sugar

2 teaspoons ground cinnamon

2 ounces unsalted butter, melted until browned

DIRECTIONS:

1. In a large mixing bowl whisk together 2 cups flour, sugar, yeast, and salt. Set aside.

2. Whisk together eggs and set aside.

3. In a small saucepan, melt together milk and butter until butter has just melted. Remove from the heat and add water and vanilla extract. Let mixture stand for a minute or two, or until the mixture registers 115 to 125 degrees F.

4. Pour the milk mixture into the dry ingredients and mix with a spatula. Add the eggs and stir the mixture until the eggs are incorporated into the batter. The eggs will feel soupy and it'll seem like the dough and the eggs are never going to come together. Keep stirring. Add the remaining ¾ cup of flour and stir with the spatula for about 2 minutes. The mixture will be sticky. That's just right.

5. Place the dough is a large, greased bowl. Cover with plastic wrap and a clean kitchen towel. Place in a warm space and allow to rest until doubled in size, about 1 hour. *The dough can be risen until doubled in size, then refrigerated overnight for use in the morning. If you're using this method, just let the dough rest on the counter for 30 minutes before following the roll-out directions below.

6. While the dough rises, whisk together the sugar and cinnamon for the filling. Set aside. Melt 2 ounces of butter in a saucepan until browned. Set aside. Grease and flour a 9x5x3-inch loaf pan. Set that aside too.

7. Deflate the risen dough and knead the remaining 2 tablespoons of flour into the dough. Cover with a clean kitchen towel and let rest for 5 minutes. On a lightly floured work surface, use a rolling pin to roll the dough out. The dough should be 12-inches tall and about 20-inches long. Use a pastry brush to spread melted butter across all of the dough. Sprinkle with all of the sugar and cinnamon mixture.

8. Slice the dough vertically, into six equal-sized strips. Stack the strips on top of one another and slice the stack into six equal slices once again. You'll have six stacks of six squares. Layer the dough squares in the loaf pan like a flip-book. Place a kitchen towel over the loaf pan and allow in a warm place for 30 to 45 minutes or until almost doubled in size.

9. Preheat oven to 350 degrees F. Place loaf in the oven and bake for 30 to 35 minutes, until the top is very golden brown. The top

may be lightly browned, but the center may still be raw. A nice, dark, golden brown will ensure that the center is cooked as well.

10. Remove from the oven and allow to rest for 20 to 30 minutes. Run a butter knife around the edges of the pan to loosen the bread and invert onto a clean board. Place a cake stand or cake plate on top of the upside down loaf, and carefully invert so it's right side up. Serve warm with coffee or tea.

11. The bread is best served the day it's made, but it can also we wrapped and kept at room temperature for up to 2 days.

CHOCOLATE CHIP ORANGE ZUCCHINI BREAD

Ingredients

3 eggs 2 cups white sugar 1 cup vegetable oil 2 teaspoons vanilla extract 2 cups grated zucchini 1 cup chopped walnuts 1 cup semisweet chocolate chips 1 tablespoon orange zest 3 cups all-purpose flour 1/4 teaspoon baking powder 1 teaspoon baking soda 1 teaspoon salt 1/2 teaspoon ground cinnamon 1 teaspoon ground nutmeg

Directions

Sift together flour, baking powder, soda, salt, and spices.

In a large bowl, beat eggs until light and fluffy. Add sugar, and continue beating until well blended. Stir in oil, vanilla, zucchini, nuts, chocolate chips, and orange rind. Blend in sifted ingredients. Turn batter into two greased 9 x 5 inch loaf pans.

Bake at 350 degrees F (175 degrees C) for 50 minutes, or until bread tests done. Remove loaves from pans, and cool. Chill before slicing.

MANAAEESH FLATBREAD

INGREDIENTS

1 (.25 ounce) package active dry yeast 3/4 cup warm water - 110 degrees F (43 degrees C) 1/4 cup olive oil 2 cups all-purpose flour 1/2 teaspoon kosher salt 1/4 cup olive oil, divided 1/4 cup za'atar 3/4 teaspoon kosher salt

Directions

Mix yeast with warm water in a large mixing bowl and allow to stand until a creamy layer of foam appears, about 10 minutes. Whisk in 1/4 cup olive oil, then gradually stir in flour and 1/2 teaspoon kosher salt.

Transfer dough to a floured surface and knead until smooth and just a little bit sticky, 10 to 12 minutes. Place dough into an oiled bowl and turn dough around in bowl to coat surface with oil; cover bowl and refrigerate dough overnight. (Dough should double in size.)

Coat a 9x13-inch baking sheet generously with 2 tablespoons olive oil; place dough in the center of the baking sheet and flatten into a thick disk. Cover dough with plastic wrap and let double in size, about 1 1/2 hours.

Use your palms and fingers to gently press and stretch dough to the edges of the oiled baking sheet, making the flatbread as even in thickness as you can. With fingertips, make small indentations in the dough. Brush dough with remaining 2 tablespoons olive oil.

Stir za'atar and 3/4 teaspoon kosher salt together in a small bowl and sprinkle evenly over the flatbread. Let dough rest for 30 minutes uncovered.

Preheat oven to 375 degrees F (190 degrees C).

Bake flatbread in the preheated oven until golden brown, 15 to 20 minutes.

MIRIAM'S NOT-SO-SECRET CHALLAH

Ingredients

2 cups water 1/2 cup margarine 7 cups bread flour, divided 1/4 cup white sugar 1/4 cup brown sugar 3 (.25 ounce) packages active dry yeast 1 tablespoon salt 4 eggs 1 egg, beaten 1 tablespoon poppy seeds

Directions

In a small saucepan, combine water and margarine in a small saucepan. Heat until margarine is melted and very warm, but not boiling.

In a large bowl, mix together 3 cups flour, white sugar, brown sugar, yeast and salt. Add water and margarine mixture; beat well. Add 4 eggs, one at a time, beating well after each addition. Stir in the remaining flour, 1/2 cup at a time, beating well after each addition. When the dough has pulled together, turn it out onto a lightly floured surface and knead until smooth and elastic, about 8 minutes.

Lightly oil a large bowl, place the dough in the bowl and turn to coat with oil. Cover with a damp cloth and let rise in a warm place until doubled in volume, about 1 hour.

Deflate the dough and turn it out onto a lightly floured surface. Divide the dough into six equal pieces and form into long 'ropes'. Braid the pieces together to form two large loaves. Place the loaves on two lightly greased cookie sheets, cover the loaves with a damp cloth and let rise until doubled in volume, about 40 minutes.

Preheat oven to 350 degrees F (175 degrees C).

Brush the risen loaves with the beaten egg and sprinkle with poppy seeds. Bake in preheated oven for 45 minutes, until loaf sounds hollow when tapped.

BETTY LATVALA

Ingredients

1 1/2 cups all-purpose flour 1 1/2 cups whole wheat flour 4 1/2 teaspoons baking powder 1 1/2 teaspoons salt 1/3 cup packed brown sugar 1 (12 fluid ounce) can or bottle beer

Directions

Preheat oven to 350 degrees F (175 degrees C). Lightly grease a 9x5 inch loaf pan.

In a large mixing bowl, combine all-purpose flour, whole wheat flour, baking powder, salt and brown sugar. Pour in beer, stir until a stiff batter is formed. It may be necessary to mix dough with your hands. Scrape dough into prepared loaf pan.

Bake in preheated oven for 50 to 60 minutes, until a toothpick inserted into center of the loaf comes out clean.

HONEY CORNBREAD

Ingredients

1 cup all-purpose flour 1 cup yellow cornmeal 1/4 cup white sugar 1 tablespoon baking powder 1 cup heavy cream 1/4 cup vegetable oil 1/4 cup honey 2 eggs, lightly beaten

Directions

Preheat oven to 400 degrees F (200 degrees C). Lightly grease a 9x9 inch baking pan.

In a large bowl, stir together flour, cornmeal, sugar and baking powder. Make a well in the center of the dry ingredients. Add the cream, oil, honey and eggs; stir to combine. Pour batter into prepared baking pan.

Bake in preheated oven for 20 to 25 minutes, until a toothpick inserted into center of pan comes out clean.

STRAWBERRY BREAD

Ingredients

2 cups fresh strawberries 3 1/8 cups all-purpose flour 2 cups white sugar 1 tablespoon ground cinnamon 1 teaspoon salt 1 teaspoon baking soda 1 1/4 cups vegetable oil 4 eggs, beaten 1 1/4 cups chopped pecans

Directions

Preheat oven to 350 degrees F (175 degrees C). Butter and flour two 9 x 5-inch loaf pans.

Slice strawberries and place in medium-sized bowl. Sprinkle lightly with sugar, and set aside while preparing batter.

Combine flour, sugar, cinnamon, salt and baking soda in large bowl; mix well. Blend oil and eggs into strawberries. Add strawberry mixture to flour mixture, blending until dry ingredients are just moistened. Stir in pecans. Divide batter into pans.

Bake in preheated oven until a tester inserted in the center comes out clean, 45 to 50 minutes (test each loaf separately). Let cool in pans on wire rack for 10 minutes. Turn loaves out of pans, and allow to cool before slicing.

BANANA BANANA BREAD

Ingredients

2 cups all-purpose flour 1 teaspoon baking soda 1/4 teaspoon salt 1/2 cup butter 3/4 cup brown sugar 2 eggs, beaten 2 1/3 cups mashed overripe bananas

Directions

Preheat oven to 350 degrees F (175 degrees C). Lightly grease a 9x5 inch loaf pan.

In a large bowl, combine flour, baking soda and salt. In a separate bowl, cream together butter and brown sugar. Stir in eggs and mashed bananas until well blended. Stir banana mixture into flour mixture; stir just to moisten. Pour batter into prepared loaf pan.

Bake in preheated oven for 60 to 65 minutes, until a toothpick inserted into center of the loaf comes out clean. Let bread cool in pan for 10 minutes, then turn out onto a wire rack.

MOM'S ZUCCHINI BREAD

Ingredients

3 cups all-purpose flour 1 teaspoon salt 1 teaspoon baking soda 1 teaspoon baking powder 1 tablespoon ground cinnamon 3 eggs 1 cup vegetable oil 2 1/4 cups white sugar 3 teaspoons vanilla extract 2 cups grated zucchini 1 cup chopped walnuts

Directions

Grease and flour two 8 x 4 inch pans. Preheat oven to 325 degrees F (165 degrees C).

Sift flour, salt, baking powder, soda, and cinnamon together in a bowl.

Beat eggs, oil, vanilla, and sugar together in a large bowl. Add sifted ingredients to the creamed mixture, and beat well. Stir in zucchini and nuts until well combined. Pour batter into prepared pans.

Bake for 40 to 60 minutes, or until tester inserted in the center comes out clean. Cool in pan on rack for 20 minutes. Remove bread from pan, and completely cool.

JANET'S RICH BANANA BREAD

Ingredients

1/2 cup butter, melted 1 cup white sugar 2 eggs 1 teaspoon vanilla extract 1 1/2 cups all-purpose flour 1 teaspoon baking soda 1/2 teaspoon salt 1/2 cup sour cream 1/2 cup chopped walnuts 2 medium bananas, sliced

Directions

Preheat oven to 350 degrees F (175 degrees C). Grease a 9x5 inch loaf pan.

In a large bowl, stir together the melted butter and sugar. Add the eggs and vanilla, mix well. Combine the flour, baking soda and salt, stir into the butter mixture until smooth. Finally, fold in the sour cream, walnuts and bananas. Spread evenly into the prepared pan.

Bake at 350 degrees F (175 degrees C) for 60 minutes, or until a toothpick inserted into the center of the loaf comes out clean. Cool loaf in the pan for 10 minutes before removing to a wire rack to cool completely.

DOWNEAST MAINE PUMPKIN BREAD

Ingredients

1 (15 ounce) can pumpkin puree 4 eggs 1 cup vegetable oil 2/3 cup water 3 cups white sugar 3 1/2 cups all-purpose flour 2 teaspoons baking soda 1 1/2 teaspoons salt 1 teaspoon ground cinnamon 1 teaspoon ground nutmeg 1/2 teaspoon ground cloves 1/4 teaspoon ground ginger

Directions

Preheat oven to 350 degrees F (175 degrees C). Grease and flour three 7x3 inch loaf pans.

In a large bowl, mix together pumpkin puree, eggs, oil, water and sugar until well blended. In a separate bowl, whisk together the flour, baking soda, salt, cinnamon, nutmeg, cloves and ginger. Stir the dry ingredients into the pumpkin mixture until just blended. Pour into the prepared pans.

Bake for about 50 minutes in the preheated oven. Loaves are done when toothpick inserted in center comes out clean.

GRANDMOTHER'S BUTTERMILK CORNBREAD

Ingredients

1/2 cup butter 2/3 cup white sugar 2 eggs 1 cup buttermilk 1/2 teaspoon baking soda 1 cup cornmeal 1 cup all-purpose flour 1/2 teaspoon salt

Directions

Preheat oven to 375 degrees F (175 degrees C). Grease an 8 inch square pan.

Melt butter in large skillet. Remove from heat and stir in sugar. Quickly add eggs and beat until well blended. Combine buttermilk with baking soda and stir into mixture in pan. Stir in cornmeal, flour, and salt until well blended and few lumps remain. Pour batter into the prepared pan.

Bake in the preheated oven for 30 to 40 minutes, or until a toothpick inserted in the center comes out clean.

BANANA SOUR CREAM BREAD

Ingredients

1/4 cup white sugar 1 teaspoon ground cinnamon 3/4 cup butter 3 cups white sugar 3 eggs 6 very ripe bananas, mashed 1 (16 ounce) container sour cream 2 teaspoons vanilla extract 2 teaspoons ground cinnamon 1/2 teaspoon salt 3 teaspoons baking soda 4 1/2 cups all-purpose flour 1 cup chopped walnuts (optional)

Directions

Preheat oven to 300 degrees F (150 degrees C). Grease four 7x3 inch loaf pans. In a small bowl, stir together 1/4 cup white sugar and 1 teaspoon cinnamon. Dust pans lightly with cinnamon and sugar mixture.

In a large bowl, cream butter and 3 cups sugar. Mix in eggs, mashed bananas, sour cream, vanilla and cinnamon. Mix in salt, baking soda and flour. Stir in nuts. Divide into prepared pans.

Bake for 1 hour, until a toothpick inserted in center comes out clean.

AMISH WHITE BREAD

Ingredients

2 cups warm water (110 degrees F/45 degrees C) 2/3 cup white sugar 1 1/2 tablespoons active dry yeast 1 1/2 teaspoons salt 1/4 cup vegetable oil 6 cups bread flour

Directions

In a large bowl, dissolve the sugar in warm water, and then stir in yeast. Allow to proof until yeast resembles a creamy foam.

Mix salt and oil into the yeast. Mix in flour one cup at a time. Knead dough on a lightly floured surface until smooth. Place in a well oiled bowl, and turn dough to coat. Cover with a damp cloth. Allow to rise until doubled in bulk, about 1 hour.

Punch dough down. Knead for a few minutes, and divide in half. Shape into loaves, and place into two well oiled 9x5 inch loaf pans. Allow to rise for 30 minutes, or until dough has risen 1 inch above pans.

Bake at 350 degrees F (175 degrees C) for 30 minutes.

CHEF JOHN'S CUBAN BREAD

Ingredients

Starter: 1/2 teaspoon active dry yeast 1/2 cup warm water 1/2 cup flour Dough: 1 package active dry yeast 2 teaspoons white sugar 3/4 cup warm water 3 tablespoons lard 2 teaspoons fine salt 3 cups all-purpose flour, or as needed - divided 1 tablespoon cornmeal Water to spray tops of loaves

Directions

Combine 1/2 cup warm water, 1/2 teaspoon yeast, and 1/2 cup flour in a bowl or measuring cup. Whisk the starter until well blended. Cover with plastic wrap and refrigerate overnight.

Place 1 package active dry yeast and 2 teaspoons sugar in a mixing bowl. Pour in 3/4 cup warm water. Let rest 15 minutes to ensure yeast is alive (bubbles will form on surface). Add lard and salt to bowl; add 1 cup of the flour. Mix until all ingredients are incorporated and dough forms a sticky ball. Add the starter (reserving 1/4 cup if you want to keep the starter going, if desired. Otherwise add it all.). Sprinkle most of the rest of the flour on the dough, reserving 1/2 cup to be used if needed when kneading.

Turn dough out onto a lightly floured work surface and knead until dough comes together in a firm ball, adding additional flour only as needed. Dough should be soft and supple with just a bit of tackiness on the surface.

Place dough in a bowl and coat surface with a little vegetable oil. Cover bowl with a damp kitchen towel and place in a warm spot to rise. Let rise until at least doubled in size, about 2 hours.

Line two rimmed baking sheets with parchment paper and sprinkle with a little cornmeal.

Transfer dough onto lightly floured surface. Lightly press the dough into a rectangle with your lightly floured hands. Divide dough in half and press and shape each half into a long 1/2-inch thick rectangle about 12 inches long. Roll up tightly starting at the long end to form a skinny loaf. Flatten a bit. Transfer each loaf to a prepared baking sheet and dust with a bit of flour. Cover with a light, dry towel and let rise until doubled in size, 1 1/2 to 2 hours.

Preheat oven to 400 degrees F (200 degrees C). Cut a 1/4-inch deep slit down the top of the loaves with a sharp knife or razor. Mist loaves lightly with water.

Place pans in pre-heated oven, one pan on lower rack, one on higher rack. After 10 minutes, switch pan positions. Continue to bake until loaves are golden brown, 10 to 15 minutes longer. Transfer loaves to cooling rack and let cool to room temperature before slicing.

GOLDEN SWEET CORNBREAD

Ingredients

1 cup all-purpose flour 1 cup yellow cornmeal 2/3 cup white sugar 1 teaspoon salt 3 1/2 teaspoons baking powder 1 egg 1 cup milk 1/3 cup vegetable oil Add all ingredients to list

Directions

Preheat oven to 400 degrees F (200 degrees C). Spray or lightly grease a 9 inch round cake pan.

In a large bowl, combine flour, cornmeal, sugar, salt and baking powder. Stir in egg, milk and vegetable oil until well combined. Pour batter into prepared pan.

Bake in preheated oven for 20 to 25 minutes, or until a toothpick inserted into the center of the loaf comes out clean.

BEST BREAD MACHINE BREAD

Ingredients

1 cup warm water (110 degrees F/45 degrees C) 2 tablespoons white sugar 1 (.25 ounce) package bread machine yeast 1/4 cup vegetable oil 3 cups bread flour 1 teaspoon salt

Directions

Place the water, sugar and yeast in the pan of the bread machine. Let the yeast dissolve and foam for 10 minutes. Add the oil, flour and salt to the yeast. Select Basic or White Bread setting, and press Start.

PUMPKIN BREAD IV

Ingredients

3 cups canned pumpkin puree 1 1/2 cups vegetable oil 4 cups white sugar 6 eggs 4 3/4 cups all-purpose flour 1 1/2 teaspoons baking powder 1 1/2 teaspoons baking soda 1 1/2 teaspoons salt 1 1/2 teaspoons ground cinnamon 1 1/2 teaspoons ground nutmeg 1 1/2 teaspoons ground cloves

Directions

Preheat the oven to 350 degrees F (175 degrees C). Grease and flour three 9x5 inch loaf pans.

In a large bowl, mix together the pumpkin, oil, sugar, and eggs. Combine the flour, baking powder, baking soda, salt, cinnamon, nutmeg, and cloves; stir into the pumpkin mixture until well blended. Divide the batter evenly between the prepared pans.

Bake in preheated oven for 45 minutes to 1 hour. The top of the loaf should spring back when lightly pressed.

EXTREME BANANA NUT BREAD 'EBNB'

Ingredients

2 cups all-purpose flour 1 teaspoon salt 2 teaspoons baking soda 1 cup butter or margarine 2 cups white sugar 2 cups mashed overripe bananas 4 eggs, beaten 1 cup chopped walnuts

Directions

Preheat the oven to 350 degrees F (175 degrees C). Grease and flour two 9x5 inch loaf pans.

Sift the flour, salt and baking soda into a large bowl. In a separate bowl, mix together the butter or margarine and sugar until smooth. Stir in the bananas, eggs, and walnuts until well blended. Pour the wet ingredients into the dry mixture, and stir just until blended. Divide the batter evenly between the two loaf pans.

Bake for 60 to 70 minutes in the preheated oven, until a knife inserted into the crown of the loaf comes out clean. Let the loaves cool in the pans for at least 5 minutes, then turn out onto a cooling rack, and cool completely. Wrap in aluminum foil to keep in the moisture. Ideally, refrigerate the loaves for 2 hours or more before serving.

SIMPLE WHOLE WHEAT BREAD

Ingredients

3 cups warm water (110 degrees F/45 degrees C) 2 (.25 ounce) packages active dry yeast 1/3 cup honey 5 cups bread flour 3 tablespoons butter, melted 1/3 cup honey 1 tablespoon salt 3 1/2 cups whole wheat flour 2 tablespoons butter, melted

Directions

In a large bowl, mix warm water, yeast, and 1/3 cup honey. Add 5 cups white bread flour, and stir to combine. Let set for 30 minutes, or until big and bubbly.

Mix in 3 tablespoons melted butter, 1/3 cup honey, and salt. Stir in 2 cups whole wheat flour. Flour a flat surface and knead with whole wheat flour until not real sticky - just pulling away from the counter, but still sticky to touch. This may take an additional 2 to 4 cups of whole wheat flour. Place in a greased bowl, turning once to coat the surface of the dough. Cover with a dishtowel. Let rise in a warm place until doubled.

Punch down, and divide into 3 loaves. Place in greased 9 x 5 inch loaf pans, and allow to rise until dough has topped the pans by one inch.

Bake at 350 degrees F (175 degrees C) for 25 to 30 minutes; do not overbake. Lightly brush the tops of loaves with 2 tablespoons melted butter or margarine when done to prevent crust from getting hard. Cool completely

PUMPKIN GINGERBREAD

Ingredients

3 cups sugar 1 cup vegetable oil 4 eggs 2/3 cup water 1 (15 ounce) can pumpkin puree 2 teaspoons ground ginger 1 teaspoon ground allspice 1 teaspoon ground cinnamon 1 teaspoon ground cloves 3 1/2 cups all-purpose flour 2 teaspoons baking soda 1 1/2 teaspoons salt 1/2 teaspoon baking powder

Directions

Preheat oven to 350 degrees F (175 degrees C). Lightly grease two 9x5 inch loaf pans.

In a large mixing, combine sugar, oil and eggs; beat until smooth. Add water and beat until well blended. Stir in pumpkin, ginger, allspice cinnamon, and clove.

In medium bowl, combine flour, soda, salt, and baking powder. Add dry ingredients to pumpkin mixture and blend just until all ingredients are mixed. Divide batter between prepared pans.

Bake in preheated oven until toothpick comes out clean, about 1 hour.

FRENCH BREAD ROLLS TO DIE FOR

Ingredients

1 1/2 cups warm water (110 degrees F/45 degrees C) 1 tablespoon active dry yeast 2 tablespoons white sugar 2 tablespoons vegetable oil 1 teaspoon salt 4 cups bread flour

Directions

In a large bowl, stir together warm water, yeast, and sugar. Let stand until creamy, about 10 minutes.

To the yeast mixture, add the oil, salt, and 2 cups flour. Stir in the remaining flour, 1/2 cup at a time, until the dough has pulled away from the sides of the bowl. Turn out onto a lightly floured surface, and knead until smooth and elastic, about 8 minutes. Lightly oil a large bowl, place the dough in the bowl, and turn to coat. Cover with a damp cloth, and let rise in a warm place until doubled in volume, about 1 hour.

Deflate the dough, and turn it out onto a lightly floured surface. Divide the dough into 16 equal pieces, and form into round balls. Place on lightly greased baking sheets at least 2 inches apart. Cover the rolls with a damp cloth, and let rise until doubled in volume, about 40 minutes. Meanwhile, preheat oven to 400 degrees F (200 degrees C).

Bake for 18 to 20 minutes in the preheated oven, or until golden brown.

AMAZINGLY EASY IRISH SODA BREAD

Ingredients

4 cups all-purpose flour 4 tablespoons white sugar 1 teaspoon baking soda 1 tablespoon baking powder 1/2 teaspoon salt 1/2 cup margarine, softened 1 cup buttermilk 1 egg 1/4 cup butter, melted 1/4 cup buttermilk

Directions

Preheat oven to 375 degrees F (190 degrees C). Lightly grease a large baking sheet.

In a large bowl, mix together flour, sugar, baking soda, baking powder, salt and margarine. Stir in 1 cup of buttermilk and egg. Turn dough out onto a lightly floured surface and knead slightly. Form dough into a round and place on prepared baking sheet. In a small bowl, combine melted butter with 1/4 cup buttermilk; brush loaf with this mixture. Use a sharp knife to cut an 'X' into the top of the loaf.

Bake in preheated oven until a toothpick inserted into the center of the loaf comes out clean, 45 to 50 minutes. Check for doneness after 30 minutes. You may continue to brush the loaf with the butter mixture while it bakes.

FOCACCIA BREAD

Ingredients

2 3/4 cups all-purpose flour 1 teaspoon salt 1 teaspoon white sugar 1 tablespoon active dry yeast 1 teaspoon garlic powder 1 teaspoon dried oregano 1 teaspoon dried thyme 1/2 teaspoon dried basil 1 pinch ground black pepper 1 tablespoon vegetable oil 1 cup water 2 tablespoons olive oil 1 tablespoon grated Parmesan cheese 1 cup mozzarella

Directions

In a large bowl, stir together the flour, salt, sugar, yeast, garlic powder, oregano, thyme, basil and black pepper. Mix in the vegetable oil and water.

When the dough has pulled together, turn it out onto a lightly floured surface, and knead until smooth and elastic. Lightly oil a large bowl, place the dough in the bowl, and turn to coat with oil. Cover with a damp cloth, and let rise in a warm place for 20 minutes.

Preheat oven to 450 degrees F (230 degrees C). Punch dough down; place on greased baking sheet. Pat into a 1/2 inch thick rectangle. Brush top with olive oil. Sprinkle with Parmesan cheese and mozzarella cheese.

Bake in preheated oven for 15 minutes, or until golden brown. Serve warm.

ABSOLUTE MEXICAN CORNBREAD

Ingredients

1 cup butter, melted 1 cup white sugar 4 eggs 1 (15 ounce) can cream-style corn 1/2 (4 ounce) can chopped green chili peppers, drained 1/2 cup shredded Monterey Jack cheese 1/2 cup shredded Cheddar cheese 1 cup all-purpose flour 1 cup yellow cornmeal 4 teaspoons baking powder 1/4 teaspoon salt

Directions

Preheat oven to 300 degrees F (150 degrees C). Lightly grease a 9x13 inch baking dish.

In a large bowl, beat together butter and sugar. Beat in eggs one at a time. Blend in cream corn, chiles, Monterey Jack and Cheddar cheese.

In a separate bowl, stir together flour, cornmeal, baking powder and salt. Add flour mixture to corn mixture; stir until smooth. Pour batter into prepared pan.

Bake in preheated oven for 1 hour, until a toothpick inserted into center of the pan comes out clean.

IRRESISTIBLE IRISH SODA BREAD

Ingredients

3 cups all-purpose flour 1 tablespoon baking powder 1/3 cup white sugar 1 teaspoon salt 1 teaspoon baking soda 1 egg, lightly beaten 2 cups buttermilk 1/4 cup butter, melted

Directions

Preheat oven to 325 degrees F (165 degrees C). Grease a 9x5 inch loaf pan.

Combine flour, baking powder, sugar, salt and baking soda. Blend egg and buttermilk together, and add all at once to the flour mixture. Mix just until moistened. Stir in butter. Pour into prepared pan.

Bake for 65 to 70 minutes, or until a toothpick inserted in the bread comes out clean. Cool on a wire rack. Wrap in foil for several hours, or overnight, for best flavor.

CATHY'S BANANA BREAD

Ingredients

1 cup mashed bananas 1 cup sour cream 1/4 cup margarine 1 1/3 cups white sugar 2 eggs 1 teaspoon vanilla extract 2 cups all-purpose flour 1 teaspoon baking soda 1 teaspoon baking powder 1/4 teaspoon salt Add all ingredients to list

Directions

Preheat oven to 350 degrees F (175 degrees C). Grease and flour one 9x13 inch pan, or two 7x3 inch loaf pans.

Combine banana and sour cream. Set aside. In a large bowl, cream together the margarine and sugar until smooth. Beat in the eggs one at a time, then stir in the vanilla and banana mixture. Combine the flour, baking soda, baking powder and salt; stir into the banana mixture. Spread the batter evenly into the prepared pan or pans.

Bake for 50 minutes in the preheated oven, or until a toothpick inserted into the center of the bread comes out clean.

CHOCOLATE BANANA BREAD

Ingredients

1 cup margarine, softened 2 cups white sugar 4 eggs 6 bananas, mashed 2 teaspoons vanilla extract 3 cups all-purpose flour 2 teaspoons baking soda 1/4 cup unsweetened cocoa powder 1 cup lite sour cream 1 cup semisweet chocolate chips Add all ingredients to list

Directions

Preheat oven to 350 degrees F (175 degrees C). Lightly grease two 9x5 inch loaf pans.

In a large bowl, cream together margarine, sugar and eggs. Stir in bananas and vanilla. Sift in flour, baking soda and cocoa; mix well. Blend in sour cream and chocolate chips. Pour batter into prepared pans.

Bake in preheated oven for 60 minutes, or until a toothpick inserted into center of a loaf comes out clean.

FRENCH BREAD

Ingredients

6 cups all-purpose flour 2 1/2 (.25 ounce) packages active dry yeast 1 1/2 teaspoons salt 2 cups warm water (110 degrees F/45 degrees C) 1 tablespoon cornmeal 1 egg white 1 tablespoon water

Directions

In a large bowl, combine 2 cups flour, yeast and salt. Stir in 2 cups warm water, and beat until well blended using a stand mixer with a dough hook attachment. Using a wooden spoon, stir in as much of the remaining flour as you can.

On a lightly floured surface, knead in enough flour to make a stiff dough that is smooth and elastic. Knead for about 8 to 10 minutes total. Shape into a ball. Place dough in a greased bowl, and turn once. Cover, and let rise in a warm place until doubled.

Punch dough down, and divide in half. Turn out onto a lightly floured surface. Cover, and let rest for 10 minutes. Roll each half into large rectangle. Roll up, starting from a long side. Moisten edge with water and seal. Taper ends.

Grease a large baking sheet. Sprinkle with cornmeal. Place loaves, seam side down, on the prepared baking sheet. Lightly beat the egg white with 1 tablespoon of water, and brush on. Cover with a damp cloth. Let rise until nearly doubled, 35 to 40 minutes.

With a very sharp knife, make 3 or 4 diagonal cuts about 1/4 inch deep across top of each loaf. Bake in a preheated 375 degrees F (190 degrees C) oven for 20 minutes. Brush again with egg white mixture. Bake for an additional 15 to 20 minutes, or until bread tests done. If necessary, cover loosely with foil to prevent over browning. Remove from baking sheet, and cool on a wire rack.

STRAWBERRY BREAD

Ingredients

2 cups fresh strawberries 3 1/8 cups all-purpose flour 2 cups white sugar 1 tablespoon ground cinnamon 1 teaspoon salt 1 teaspoon baking soda 1 1/4 cups vegetable oil 4 eggs, beaten 1 1/4 cups chopped pecans

Directions

Preheat oven to 350 degrees F (175 degrees C). Butter and flour two 9 x 5-inch loaf pans.

Slice strawberries and place in medium-sized bowl. Sprinkle lightly with sugar, and set aside while preparing batter.

Combine flour, sugar, cinnamon, salt and baking soda in large bowl; mix well. Blend oil and eggs into strawberries. Add strawberry mixture to flour mixture, blending until dry ingredients are just moistened. Stir in pecans. Divide batter into pans.

Bake in preheated oven until a tester inserted in the center comes out clean, 45 to 50 minutes (test each loaf separately). Let cool in pans on wire rack for 10 minutes. Turn loaves out of pans, and allow to cool before slicing.

CINNAMON BREAD

Ingredients

2 cups all-purpose flour 1 cup white sugar 2 teaspoons baking powder 1/2 teaspoon baking soda 1 1/2 teaspoons ground cinnamon 1 teaspoon salt 1 cup buttermilk 1/4 cup vegetable oil 2 eggs 2 teaspoons vanilla extract 2 tablespoons white sugar 1 teaspoon ground cinnamon 2 teaspoons margarine

Directions

Preheat oven to 350 degrees F (175 degrees C). Grease one 9x5 inch loaf pan.

Measure flour, 1 cup sugar, baking powder, baking soda, 1 1/2 teaspoons cinnamon, salt, buttermilk, oil, eggs and vanilla into large mixing bowl. Beat 3 minutes. Pour into prepared loaf pan. Smooth top.

Combine 2 tablespoons white sugar, 1 teaspoon cinnamon and butter, mixing until crumbly. Sprinkle topping over smoothed batter. Using knife, cut in a light swirling motion to give a marbled effect.

Bake for about 50 minutes. Test with toothpick. When inserted it should come out clean. Remove bread from pan to rack to cool.

CREAMY BANANA BREAD

Ingredients

1/2 cup margarine, softened 1 (8 ounce) package cream cheese, softened 1 1/4 cups white sugar 2 eggs 1 cup mashed bananas 1 teaspoon vanilla extract 2 1/4 cups all-purpose flour 1 1/2 teaspoons baking powder 1/2 teaspoon baking soda 3/4 cup chopped pecans 2 tablespoons brown sugar 2 teaspoons ground cinnamon

Directions

Preheat oven to 350 degrees F (175 degrees C). Grease and flour two 8x4-inch loaf pans.

Cream the margarine and cream cheese together. Gradually add the white sugar, and continue beating until light and fluffy. Add eggs one at a time, beating well after each addition. Stir in the mashed bananas and vanilla. Add flour, baking powder, and baking soda; mix until batter is just moist.

In a small bowl, mix together chopped pecans, 2 tablespoons brown sugar, and cinnamon.

Divide half the batter between the two prepared loaf pans. Sprinkle pecan mixture over the batter in the pans, and top with remaining batter.

Bake in the preheated oven until a toothpick inserted in the center of each loaf comes out clean, about 45 minutes.

BRIOCHE ROLLS WITH CHOCOLATE

Ingredients

1 pound Brioche dough*

1/4 cup semisweet chocolate chips, chopped chocolate or Nutella

Egg Wash

1 large egg yolk

1 Tbsp water

Turbinado sugar

Directions

Line a baking sheet with parchment paper. Flour board or counter well and dust dough with flour. Use floured hands to quickly shape into a ball by stretching the surface of the dough around to the bottom on all four sides, rotating dough as you go.

Use a floured bench scraper to cut dough into eight 2-ounce portions. Spoon a teaspoon of chocolate or Nutella in the center of each portion; pinch ends to seal. Flip rolls over (seam-side down) and use bench scraper to shape into a round. Place rolls two inches apart on baking sheet; cover loosely with plastic wrap and let rest at room temperature for 40 minutes. In the last 20 minutes, preheat oven to 350°F.

Whisk egg yolk and water together in a small bowl; use a pastry brush to gently glaze the top of the rolls; sprinkle with turbinado sugar. Bake for 20 minutes, until rolls are deep golden. Cool for 2 minutes on baking sheet, then transfer to a wire rack to cool slightly before serving.

OUTBACK STEAKHOUSE COPYCAT HONEY WHEAT BREAD

Ingredients

2 ½ c .warm water 100°-110°F

1/4 c .vegetable oil

2 T .caramel color

1/2 c .honey

3 ½ c .whole-wheat flour

2 T .cocoa

2 T .active dry yeast

1 tsp .salt

2-3 c .bread flour

rolled oats for dusting loaves

Instructions

In the bowl of a stand mixer fitter with a dough hook, stir together water, oil, caramel color, and honey until mixed well.

Add wheat flour to water mixture.

Add cocoa, yeast, and salt, and stir until blended.

Allow mixture sit for 10 minutes.

Stir in bread flour, one cup at a time, until dough clings to hook and almost clears the sides of mixer, about 3-4 minutes.

Cover bowl with greased plastic wrap.

Allow dough to rise in the bowl until doubled, about 30-60 minutes.

Divide into 2 pieces.

Cover each piece with greased plastic wrap, and let dough rest for 5 minutes.

Shape pieces into loaves, and sprinkle with oats.

Place each loaf in a greased 9x5-inch loaf pan.

Let dough rise until doubled, about 30-60 minutes.

Toward the end of the rising time, preheat oven to 350 F.

Bake at for 30-40 minutes.

SWEET POTATO CHALLAH

Ingredients

1 1/4 cups warm water (110 degrees F/45 degrees C)

1 tablespoon active dry yeast

1/2 cup honey

2 tablespoons melted butter

1 whole egg plus 2 yolks

2 teaspoons salt

4-6 cups unbleached all-purpose flour

1 cup cooked, mashed sweet potatoes

egg wash, (1 beaten egg plus 1 tablespoon water)

Directions

In a large bowl, dissolve yeast in warm water. Mix in honey, butter, egg and yolks, mashed sweet potatoes and salt. Add the flour one cup at a time, beating after each addition, graduating to kneading with hands as dough thickens. Knead until smooth and elastic and no longer sticky, adding flour as needed. Cover with a damp clean cloth and let rise for 1 1/2 hours or until dough has doubled in bulk.

Punch down the risen dough and turn out onto floured board. Divide in half and knead each half for five minutes or so, adding flour as needed to keep from getting sticky. Form dough into desired shapes. I formed mine into 6 strand braids.

Grease two baking trays and place finished braid or round on each. Cover with towel and let rise about one hour. Preheat oven to 350 degrees F (190 degrees C). Beat one egg with 1 tablespoon of water and brush a generous amount over each braid.

Bake at 350 degrees F (190 degrees C) for about 25 minutes. Cool on a rack for at least one hour before slicing.

PARKER HOUSE ROLLS

Ingredients

1 envelope active dry yeast

1 cup whole milk

¼ cup vegetable shortening

3 tablespoons sugar

1½ teaspoons kosher salt

1 large egg, room temperature

3½ cups all-purpose flour, plus more for surface

Canola oil (for bowl)

¼ cup unsalted butter

Flaky sea salt

Special Equipment

13x9-inch baking dish

Preparation

Whisk yeast and ¼ cup warm water (110°-115°) in a small bowl; let stand 5 minutes.

Heat milk in a small saucepan over medium until just warm. Combine shortening, sugar, and kosher salt in a large bowl. Add warm milk; whisk to blend, breaking up shortening into small clumps (it may not melt completely). Whisk in yeast mixture and egg. Add 3½ cups flour; stir vigorously with a wooden spoon until dough forms. Knead dough with lightly floured hands on a lightly floured surface until smooth, 4–5 minutes. Transfer to a lightly oiled bowl; turn to coat. Cover loosely with plastic wrap. Let stand at room temperature until doubled, about 1½ hours.

Preheat oven to 350°. Melt butter in a small saucepan. Lightly brush baking dish with some melted butter. Punch down dough; divide into 4 equal pieces. Working with 1 piece at a time, roll out on a lightly floured surface into a 12x6" rectangle.

Cut lengthwise into three 2"-wide strips; cut each crosswise into three 4x2" rectangles. Brush half of each (about 2x2") with melted butter; fold unbuttered side over, allowing a ¼-inch overhang. Place flat in 1 corner of dish, folded edge against short side of dish. Add remaining rolls, shingling to form 1 long row. Repeat with remaining dough for 4 rows. Brush with melted butter, loosely cover with plastic, and chill at least 30 minutes or up to 6 hours.

Bake rolls until golden and puffed, 25–35 minutes. Brush with butter; sprinkle sea salt over. Serve warm.

MOM´S AMAZING SPELT BREAD ROLLS

Ingredients

1 cup (2,5 dl) whole spelt grain (soaked for at least 8 hours)

1/3 cup (¾ dl) olive oil

2 cups (5 dl) water

25 grams yeast

1 tbsp maple syrup

1 cup (2,5 dl) rolled oats

1 cup (2,5 dl) whole spelt flour

4 ¼ cups (1 liter) finely ground spelt flour

100 grams walnuts

½ cup (1 dl) sunflower seeds

½ cup (1 dl) pumpkin seeds

A pinch of salt

Direction

Cover the whole spelt grains with water, and let them soak for at least 8 hours (or overnight). Blend all the dry ingredients together in a bowl. Heat the water until it reaches body temperature, and blend it with the yeast. Add the olive oil, maple syrup and water to the bowl, and work the wet and dry ingredients together using your hands. Add the soaked whole spelt together with the water they were soaked in. When everything is well mixed, leave the dough in the bowl and cover the bowl with plastic foil and towels. Let the dough rise for about 1- 1 ½ hours. Make bread rolls, and put them on a baking tray lined with baking paper. Cover the tray and the bread rolls with towels, and let the bread rolls rest and rise for about 30 minutes. Spray some water on top of the rolls, and sprinkle with seeds. Push the seeds lightly into the rolls. Bake at 430 OF (220OC) in the middle of the oven for about 10-12 minutes, until they are golden on top.

HERB & CHEESE PULL-APART BREAD

For the bread

1 cup warm water

3 Tablespoons sugar

2 1/4 teaspoons instant yeast

2 cups bread flour

2 Tablespoons unsalted butter, melted

3/4 teaspoon salt

1 cup all-purpose flour

For the filling

1/2 stick unsalted butter, melted

3 to 4 cloves garlic, minced

3/4 cup fresh herbs, any combination that suits you

1 cup shredded cheese

salt

freshly ground black pepper

Instructions

1. In the bowl of a stand mixer fitted with the paddle attachment, combine the water, sugar, and yeast. Add the 2 cups of flour, salt, and the butter then mix until a shaggy dough is formed.

2. Switch to the dough hook, and with the mixer on low speed, add the all-purpose flour, a few tablespoons at a time, until the

dough forms. Knead 6 to 9 minutes until soft and pliable, and dough no longer sticks to the sides of the bowl.

3. Turn the dough out onto a lightly floured surface and knead to form a smooth ball. Transfer to a lightly oiled bowl and allow to rise 1 to 2 hours, or until doubled in size.

4. Punch down the dough and turn out onto a lightly floured surface. Allow to rest for 5 minutes. Meanwhile, chop the herbs and garlic, melt the butter, and grate the cheese.

5. Roll the dough out into a 12 x 20-inch rectangle. Brush with 2 tablespoons of the melted butter, then sprinkle the dough with the garlic, herbs, and cheese. Sprinkle with salt and pepper to taste.

6. Cut the dough into 6 equally-sized strips using a pizza cutter or knife. Stack the strips on top of each other and cut into 6 equally-sized squares.

7. Grease a 9 x 5-inch loaf pan, and stack the squares on top of each other in the pan. An easy way to do this is to hold the pan on its side.* If you lose some of the filling as you stack, just sprinkle it on top once the dough has been stacked. Drizzle the remaining 2 tablespoons of melted butter over the top.

8. Cover with a clean kitchen towel and allow to rise for about 40 minutes.

9. Preheat the oven to 350°F (180°C). Bake the bread 35 to 45 minutes, or until the top is golden-brown and the inside is cooked through. If the top browns too quickly, tent the bread with foil.

10. Remove from oven and allow to cool for at least 20 minutes. Run a knife around the edges and invert onto a serving platter to serve.

NO-KNEAD BREAD

Ingredients

3 cups all-purpose or bread flour, plus more for dusting (I often use half whole wheat and half all-purpose, sometimes with a shake of ground flaxseed added)

1/4 tsp. instant or regular active dry yeast

1 tsp. salt

Direction

In a large bowl stir together the flour, yeast and salt. Add 1 1/2 cups plus 2 tablespoons water, and stir until blended; dough will be shaggy and sticky. Cover bowl with plastic wrap or a plate and let it rest on the countertop for 18-24 hours at room temperature.

The dough is ready when its surface is dotted with bubbles. Flour a work surface and place dough on it; sprinkle it with a little more flour and fold it over on itself once or twice, then roughly shape into a ball. Generously coat a cotton towel (not terry cloth) with flour; put dough seam side down on towel and dust with more flour. Fold it over the bread or cover with another cotton towel and let it sit for another hour or two.

While the bread is resting, preheat the oven to 450°. Put a 6-8 quart heavy covered pot (cast iron, enamel, Pyrex or ceramic) in oven as it heats. When the dough is ready, carefully remove pot from oven. Slide your hand under towel and flip the dough over into the pot; it may look like a mess, but that's OK. Cover and bake for 30 minutes, then remove the lid and bake another 10-15 minutes, until it's nice and golden. Eat up!

PIZZA MONKEY BREAD

INGREDIENTS

2 1/4 teaspoons active dry yeast

1 cup warm water

1 teaspoon sugar

2 cups bread flour

1 cup all purpose flour

2 teaspoons salt

1/2 cup butter, melted

2/3 cup Pecorino Romano cheese, grated

3 tablespoons fresh parsley, chopped

5 scallions, chopped

10 basil leaves, chopped

5 cloves garlic, minced

Kosher salt and freshly cracked black pepper

1 cup marinara or pizza sauce

INSTRUCTIONS

In a medium bowl, combine the bread flour, all purpose flour and salt. Set aside.

Combine the active yeast and water in a mixing bowl fitted with a dough hook. Let it sit for a few minutes to make sure your yeast is working. Add the sugar and mix for a quick second. Add the flour mixture in batches, scraping down the sides of the bowl. Let the dough hook work its magic for 5-6 minutes until the dough has come together into a large mass. Remove the dough to an oiled bowl and let rise for 60 minutes.

After an hour, remove the dough from the bowl and cut into small 1/2 inch cubes. Dust with flour to prevent them from sticking together. Set aside.

Butter and flour 6 small bundt pans. (You could also use a large bundt pan)

Melt the butter in a small bowl.

Combine the cheese, herbs, salt/pepper and garlic in a large bowl. Add the melted butter and mix together with a spoon. Toss in the cut dough and make sure it all gets a coat of the butter mixture. Start layering the cubes into the bundt pans until they are 3/4 of the way full. Let sit for 30 minutes for the dough to rise a little more and while they are rising, preheat the oven to 400 degrees F.

Place bundt pans into the oven and bake for 25-30 minutes until the bread and cheese is golden brown. Serve with warmed marinara sauce or pizza sauce.

CINNAMON BUTTERMILK BREAD WREATH

Ingredients:

1 package Red Star Platinum Yeast

1 cup buttermilk

1/4 cup butter

1/4 cup sugar

1/2 tbs salt

2.5-3.5 cups King Arthur Bread Flour

Topping:

1/4 cup sugar

1 tbs cinnamon

Directions:

On your stove top add buttermilk, sugar, salt and butter together. Heat until the butter has melted. Set aside until it cools to below 110 degrees.

Meanwhile, proof your yeast. This is optional. However I find I get a much quicker rise if I do this step. Mix yeast package in 1/4 cup of water and 1/2 tsp sugar. It is "proofed" when it starts to get foamy and bubbles.

In the bowl of your electric mixer Mix yeast mixture, butter mixture and 2 cups of flour with your dough hook on medium. Slowly add more flour as needed and scrape down the sides.

Once the dough has come together. Turn you mixer up to high and allow it to "knead" the dough for 5 minutes. When the dough is smooth and elastic remove it from the mixer.

Place dough in a buttered bowl covered with a dishtowel and allow to rise until doubled in size. Depending on the brand of your yeast and temperature of your home this time varies for everyone.

Once the bread has doubled, remove from bowl and punch dough down. Cut into three equal portions and roll each into a long snake about 1 inch thick.

Braid the 3 pieces and connect the ends forming a wreath. Place on a parchment paper lined cookie sheet and allow to rise again until doubled.

While dough is rising, preheat oven to 350.

Just before place the bread in the oven. In a small bowl mix sugar and cinnamon together. Sprinkle over the top of of your bread and bake for 20-30 minutes or until the bread is golden and sounds hollow when you flick the top.

ORANGE CHOCOLATE SWIRL BREAD – LOW CARB AND GLUTEN-FREE

INGREDIENTS

CHOCOLATE SWIRL AND GLAZE

2 oz unsweetened chocolate, chopped

2 tbsp butter

2 tbsp powdered Swerve Sweetener or powdered erythritol

½ tsp vanilla extract

ORANGE BREAD

3 cups almond flour

1/3 cup unflavoured whey protein powder

1 1/2 tsp baking powder

1 tsp baking soda

1/2 tsp salt

1/2 cup butter, softened

1/2 cup granulated Swerve Sweetener or other erythritol

3 large eggs

Zest of medium orange

20 drops stevia extract

1/4 cup orange juice

1/4 cup almond milk

INSTRUCTIONS

Preheat oven to 300F and grease a loaf pan well.

In a small saucepan over low heat, melt chocolate, butter and powdered erythritol together until smooth. Stir in vanilla extract and set aside.

In a medium bowl, whisk together almond flour, protein powder, baking powder, baking soda and salt. Set aside.

In a large bowl, beat butter until smooth. Add granulated erythritol and beat until lighter and well-combined, about 2 minutes.

Beat in eggs, one at time, scraping down beaters and sides of bowl with a rubber spatula as needed.

Beat in orange zest and stevia extract.

Beat in half of the almond flour mixture, then beat in orange juice and almond milk. Beat in remaining almond flour mixture until well combined.

Spread half the batter into the prepared pan, and then dollop with about 2/3 of the chocolate glaze. Use a knife to swirl the chocolate into the batter.

Top with remaining batter, and swirl a bit more, then smooth the top.

Bake 55 to 60 minutes, or until top is deep golden brown and a tester inserted in the center comes out clean. Let cool in pan 5 minutes, then flip out onto a wire rack to cool completely.

Drizzle with remaining chocolate glaze.

HOMEMADE NAAN

Ingredients

3 cups all-purpose flour

1 cup whole wheat flour

1 teaspoon baking soda

1 1/2 teaspoons baking powder

1 tablespoon sugar

3/4 teaspoon active dry yeast

1/4 cup water (room temp or slightly above)

3/4 cup whole milk (room temp or slightly above)

1 cup plain yogurt (not Greek)

Melted butter or ghee (for brushing)

Optional toppings or add-ins: garlic, onion, herbs, cheese Combine yeast, sugar, and lukewarm water and let sit for 5 to 10 minutes, or until foamy. In the meantime, combine flours, baking powder, and baking soda in a bowl. Make a well in the center. Stir milk and yogurt together. Once the yeast mixture is foamy, stir it into the yogurt and milk. Pour into the well of the dry ingredients. Stir with a wooden spoon to combine, then knead dough until smooth. Place dough in a well-oiled bowl, cover with a tea towel or plastic wrap, and let rise for about an hour, or until doubled in size. When dough is ready, punch down and turn out on a well-floured surface. Divide in half, then divide each half into eight pieces of equal size. Roll each piece out into a thin oval approximately 6 inches long and 1/8 inch thick. Heat a cast iron skill over medium-high heat on the stove top. Once pan is hot, brush each side of the naan with melted butter/ghee. (If adding toppings like onion/garlic/spice, add them to the second side you brush with butter and gently press them into the dough.) Place dough into your skillet. (If you've adding toppings, place it topping side-up.) Let cook for around 1 minute, or until dough puffs and bubbles form on top.Flip and let cook for another minute. Repeat with remaining pieces of dough.

GRAIN-FREE SANDWICH BREAD (PALEO AND SCD)

INGREDIENTS:

1 cup smooth raw cashew butter at room temperature

4 large eggs, separated

½ to 2 tablespoons honey (use 2tbl if you plan to use if for sweeter dishes like french toast)

2.5 teaspoons apple cider vinegar

¼ cup almond milk

¼ cup coconut flour

1 teaspoon baking soda

½ teaspoon sea salt

INSTRUCTIONS:

Preheat your oven to 300 degrees. For a white colored loaf as in the photo, place a small dish of water on the bottom rack.

Line the bottom of an 8.5×4.5 glass loaf pan with parchment paper, then spread a very thin coating of coconut oil on the sides of the pan.

Beat the cashew butter with the egg yolks, then add the honey, vinegar, and milk.

Beat the egg whites in a separate bowl until peaks form.

Combine the dry ingredients in another small bowl. Sorry for all of the dishes!

Make sure your oven is completely preheated before adding the egg whites and the dry ingredients to the cashew butter mixture. You don't want your whites to fall, and the baking soda will activate once it hits the eggs and vinegar.

Pour the dry ingredients into the wet ingredients, and beat until combined. This will result in more of a wet batter than a dough. Make sure to get all of the sticky butter mixture off of the bottom of the bowl so you don't end up with clumps.

Pour the beaten egg whites into the cashew butter mixture, beating again until just combined. You don't have to be gentle with this, but don't over mix.

Pour the batter into the prepared loaf pan, then immediately put it into the oven.

Bake for 45-50 minutes, until the top is golden brown and a toothpick comes out clean. Don't be tempted to open the oven door anytime before 40 minutes, as this will allow the steam to escape and you will not get a properly risen loaf.

Remove from the oven, then let cool for 15-20 minutes. Use a knife to free the sides from the loaf pan, then flip it upside down and release the loaf onto a cooling rack. Cool right-side up for an hour before serving.

Wrap the loaf up tightly and store in the fridge for 1 week.

APPETIZING BRIOCHE BREAD WITH NO MILK NOR BUTTER

Ingredients

250 g of flour

125 g of water

1 Tbsp of dried baker's yeast

50 g of sugar

a pinch of salt

30 g of extra virgin olive oil

½ vanilla bean

icing sugar for topping

Instructions

Put the flour, yeast, water, sugar and vanilla beans into the bread machine bowl.

Knead for 5 to 6 minutes.

Add salt and olive oil.

Knead until well combined, stopping the mixer and helping the dough with a wood spoon once in a while, as the oil isn't absorbed easily.

Cover the bowl and let it rest until doubled in size.

Just touch the dough to deflate it, put into another bowl, cover with plastic wrap and let it rest in the fridge for 3 hours.

Take the dough and divide it in 10 equal pieces.

Form a ball with each one of them and put on a baking tray covered with parchment paper.

Let them double again (about 1½ hour).

Preheat the oven to 180°C and bake them for about 20 minutes or until colored.

Sprinkle some icing sugar on top.

HONEY BEER BREAD

Ingredients (one loaf):

3 cups all-purpose flour

1 tablespoon baking powder

2 tablespoons sugar

1 teaspoon salt

2 tablespoons honey

1 can beer

1/4 cup unsalted butter, melted

Directions:

Preheat oven to 350F. Grease a loaf pan. Line the bottom of the pan with parchment paper. Set aside.

In a medium bowl, whisk together the flour, sugar, baking powder and salt.

Using a wooden spoon, stir the beer and honey into the dry ingredients until just mixed. (Microwave the honey for 5 to 10 seconds beforehand to make it easier to stir in)

Pour half the melted butter into the loaf pan. Then spoon the batter into the pan, and pour the rest of the butter on top of the batter. Use a pastry brush to spread it around.

Bake for 50 to 60 minutes, until top is golden brown and a toothpick/knife inserted in the middle comes out clean.

EASY ONE-BOWL PUMPKIN BREAD

ingredients

1 cup white sugar

½ cup brown sugar

1-3/4 cups all-purpose flour

1 teaspoon baking soda

¾ teaspoon salt

1 teaspoon ground cinnamon

½ teaspoon ground nutmeg

¼ teaspoon ground cloves

⅛ teaspoon ground ginger

¾ cup pumpkin puree

2 eggs

½ cup vegetable oil (I used coconut)

⅓ cup water

1 teaspoon of vanilla

instructions

Preheat oven to 350F. Butter and flour a 9x5 loaf pan, set aside.

Whisk together sugars, flour, spices, baking soda and salt in a large bowl. Make a well in the center of the bowl. Add pumpkin, eggs, oil, water and vanilla. Whisk, starting with the wet ingredients and working your way to the outside of the bowl, mixing until batter is smooth and clump-free. (Don't over-mix)

Pour batter into the loaf pan and bake for 55-65 minutes, or until a toothpick inserted into the center comes out clean. Cool in the pan for 5 minutes and then cool on a rack until ready to serve.

ZUCCHINI AND PECAN BREAD

Ingredients

270 grams unbleached all purpose flour

1/2 tsp aluminum free baking soda

1/2 tsp aluminum free baking powder

1 tsp ground cinnamon

1/2 tsp sea salt

2 organic eggs

1/2 cup + 2 Tbs sunflower oil

150 grams sugar

115 grams peach jam

zest of half an orange

285 grams organic zucchini, grated

115 grams pecans, chopped

Demerara sugar for topping

In a large bowl, combine the flour, baking soda, baking powder, salt and cinnamon. In a separate bowl, whisk together the eggs, sugar, oil, orange zest, peach jam and grated zucchini. Add the liquid ingredients to the dry and mix until combined. Add the chopped pecans and fold.

Bake in a 350 degree oven. Check for doneness with a toothpick. If it comes out clean, they are done.

TADKA BREAD SNACK

Ingredients

2 Tbsp vegetable or olive oil

1/4 tsp mustard seeds

1 onion, peeled and chopped

2 green chillies, seeded and chopped

1/4 tsp turmeric

1/2 tsp sugar (optional)

1/4 tsp ground cumin

1/4 tsp salt

1 Tbsp yogurt

1 tsp lemon juice

4 slices bread, cubed

Fresh coriander leaves, to garnish

1 tomato, chopped

How to Make Tadka Bread Snack

Heat the oil in a small saucepan, then add the mustard seeds. Once they have popped, tip in the onion and chillies and stir for a minute.Then add the turmeric, sugar, cumin and salt and continue to fry for 1 minute. Pour in the yogurt and lemon juice, stirring continuously.Lastly, fold in the bread carefully so that it doesn't crumble too much.Cook for 2 more minutes, then serve sprinkled with coriander and chopped tomato.Tip: Dollop some extra yogurt over the finished dish to cool it.

RAGI WHEAT BREAD

Ingredients

1 cup ragiatta

1 cup whole wheat flour (atta)

100 gmgur (jaggery)

1 tsp refined oil

1/2 kg chopped spinach

Cup of curd

1 tsp baking soda

How to Make Ragi Wheat Bread

Take a bowl and put the above ingredients in it. Mix all the ingredients together till it gets consistency.Spread the mixture in a baking dish and put in oven for 40 minutes at 180 degrees.Take it out from the oven and slice evenly.

BREAD PUDDING

Ingredients

2 eggs

2 Tbsp sugar

1 tsp vanilla essence

1 to 1 1/12 cup milk

Raisins

4-5 bread slices, cut in cubes

2 -3 tsp marmalade

How to Make Bread Pudding

Break two eggs in a bowl.Whisk them till they are nice and fluffy.Add the sugar.Add essence and milk.Mix well.Sprinkle some raisinsLine a steaming dish with bread slices cut in cubes.Pour the mixture over the bread.Glaze it with some marmalade.Now put the plate onto a steamer and place it in boiling water for about 10 minutes.Alternatively you can bake it also bake it for 5-7 minutes.

TEMPERED BREAD VAGHARIA

Ingredients

5-7 whole wheat bread slices

1 tomato - finely chopped

2 stalks of curry leaves

3 green chillies - chopped 1/2 a cup of sprouts

1 tsp. sesame seeds

1/4 tsp cumin

1/4 tsp mustard seeds

1/2 tspchilli powder

1/2 tsp turmeric powder

1/2 tspasafoetida powder

1/2 lemon, juice extracted

salt to taste

2 tbsp oil

coriander leaves - for garnishing

How to Make

Crumble bread slices coarsely with hands. Sprinkle chilli powder, turmeric, salt over bread. Mix gently with hands, keep aside. Heat oil in a large pan, add seeds, asafoetida, allow to splutter. Add chillies, curry leaves, tomatoes, moong sprouts. Stir and sauté for 2-3 minutes, add lemon juice. Add bread, sesame seeds, stir gently till well blended with seasoning mixture. Sprinkle coriander leaves. Serve hot and right away.

EGGY BREAD BLT

Ingredients

6-8 rashers bacon, rinds removed

1 loaf of ciabatta or French baguette

6 eggs

2 Tbsp milk

1 Tbsp light olive oil

2 tomatoes, finely sliced

25 gm rocket leaves

1 Tbsp Dijon mustard

2 Tbsp mayonnaise

A squeeze of tomato ketchup

Salt & freshly ground black pepper for seasoning

How to Make

Cut the bread into 3 equal portions, length wise and horizontally.Crack the eggs into a bowl, add the milk, season well & beat thoroughly.Pour on to a large plate and lay the bread, cut the side down in the eggy mixture. Leave to soak for a minute before turning over.Heat a large frying pan, add oil and fry the bacon on medium heat till crisp. Remove & drain well on kitchen paper.Next, fry your eggy bread. Start with the cut side down & cook for 1-2 minute on medium heat till each piece is golden brown. Turnover and cook for another minute or so.Now place the bread on a plate & spread the ketchup on the base slices.Add a layer of tomato, followed by the bacon and the rocket leaves.Finish by spreading the Dijon mustard &mayo onto the top half of the eggy bread slices & assemble all together. Cut at an angle and serve immediately .Tip: For vegetarian could do this without bacon. Just add some fresh mozzarella cheese and maybe some caramelized onions.

BRUSCHETTA

Ingredients

1 loaf of country bread

Cloves of garlic

2 tomatoes, chopped

Basil leaves

5 Tbsp of olive oil

4 portobello mushrooms sliced

1 garlic clove grated

1 red chilli , deseeded and chopped

1 Tbsp butter

Salt and pepper, to taste

How to Make

Slice the bread into two halves from the center.Cut a clove of garlic, rub on the surface of bread and sprinkle some olive oil on it.Roast in the oven for 5 minutes.

For mushroom and garlic topping:

In a pan put butter, oil, garlic, thyme and stir.Add mushrooms, chopped chillies and toss.Add salt, pepper and cook.

For tomato and basil topping:In a bowl add chopped tomatoes, chopped basil, salt, pepper, olive oil and mix well .

To serve: Place the bread on a tray and pile up the toppings on it and serve.

OLIVE AND ROSEMARY FOCACCIA BREAD

Ingredients

2 tsp active dry yeast

1 tspreg sugar

3 cups flour/atta

1 3/4 cup lukewarm water

1 tsp salt

3 Tbsp olive oil

3/4 tsp chopped fresh rosemary or 1/2 tsp dried

1/3 cup kalmata olives pitted and cut into circles

How to Make Olive and Rosemary Focaccia Bread

Start by taking the temp of your lukewarm water. It should be 45 degrees centigrade or 110 degrees Fahrenheit.In a measuring cup put sugar. Take the right temp of water and add yeast to 3/4 cup warm water. It should start bubbling.Keep aside the water and yeast mix for 10 minutes. Now add to sugar.Add salt and rosemary to the 3 cups flour and mix with hands. Add 1.5 tablespoon olive oil to flour. Add sliced olives. Mix with hands.Now add the yeast mix to flour along with rest of water, knead to make a nice dough ball using flour if needed.Put 1 tablespoon olive oil in a bowl and rub dough ball all over with the oil. Cling film this bowl along with dough ball.Keep in a nice warm place for 1 hour so it doubles in size. Take out and roll and punch all air out.Roll and place in a nice pizza sheet with holes. Cling film again and keep in warm place for 30 minutes.Let it rise further. Now open and rub 1 tablespoon olive oil (to get a nice crispy finish).Use fingers to create the holes in focaccia and decorate with black olives or herbs.Keep in middle rack of oven at 220 degree centigrade for 35 to 40 minutes. Cool 10 minutes before serving.

BREAD DAHI VADA

Ingredients

10 bread slices

250 gm curd

Oil to fry

Salt and black pepper to taste

1/2 tsp red chilli powder

1/2 tspamchoor powder

Chopped mint leaves

A pinch of zeera powder

1 Tbspanardana

How to Make

Remove the brown portion from all slices. Soak these in water and squeeze. Then mix mashed paneer in soaked bread slices. Add a pinch of salt and amchoor. Make small-sized balls, flatten and deep fry till light brown. Remove from oil and soak in warm water for 10 minutes. Squeeze and keep aside.Beat the curd. Then add salt and chilli powder. Pour over the vadas and decorate with mint, jeera powder and anardana.

BANANA OAT BREAD

Ingredients

1 1/2 cup whole wheat flour

1/2 cup oatmeal flour

3 ripe bananas

3/4 cup dark brown sugar

1/3 cup extra light virgin olive oil

1 tsp vanilla essence

1 egg

1/2 tsp baking powder

1/4 tsp baking soda

Pinch of salt

Chopped walnuts, to garnish

How to Make

Pre-heat oven to 180 degrees Celsius.Combine all dry ingredients in a bowl (Whole wheat flour, oatmeal, baking powder, baking soda, salt,sugar).Combine all wet ingredients in a bowl (Mashed ripe bananas, Egg, vanilla essence, olive oil).Fold in dry ingredients into the wet ingredients.Lightly oil a baking tin with olive oil.Add the banana bread batter into the baking tin. Sprinkle nuts of choice. Place the baking tin in the oven and let it bake for about 50-55 mins or until a pierced toothpick comes out clean.Serve warm or cold.

STUFFED VEGETABLE BREAD

Ingredients

For the bread:

2 cups flour (atta or maida)

2 tsp yeast

1/2 warm water to knead

2 tsp olive oil

1/2 tsp salt

1/2 tsp sugar

For the filling:

3 cheese slices

1 tomato, sliced

1/2 onion, thinly sliced

1 capsicum, thinly sliced

1/2 tsp garlic

1 tsp basil

5-6 olives

1 egg white, beaten

Sesame seeds

How to Make

In a bowl add water and yeast. Let it stand for a minute.Add salt and sugar. Add the flour and olive oil.Knead it into a dough. Add more water if needed.Cover it with cling film and leave it to rest and rise to its double in a draught-free place.This should take about 1-1 1/2 hours.Once the dough has doubled, roll it out in a thickish round like the shape of a pizza.Now for the fillings, first add the cheese slices.Next add the tomatoes, onions and capsicums.Add the garlic, basil and olives.Remember to place these fillings in the middle of the dough.Fold the dough from both sides over the filling.Glaze it with some egg white.Sprinkle some sesame seeds.Place this on a greased baking sheet and into the oven at 180 degree Celsius for about 25-30 minutes till it fluffs up and becomes nice & golden.

PÃO DE QUEIJO (BRAZILIAN CHEESE BREAD)

Ingredients

1 cup whole milk

1/2 cup vegetable oil

1 teaspoon salt

10 ounces tapioca flour or sour cassava flour (about 2 cups)

2 large eggs

1 to 1 1/2 cups grated Parmesan cheese

Equipment

Medium saucepan

Wooden spoon

Standing mixer with paddle attachment (or mixing bowl and elbow grease)

2 baking sheets

Parchment paper or silicone baking mats

Instructions

Heat the oven: Arrange 2 racks to divide the oven into thirds and heat to 450°F. Line 2 baking sheets with parchment paper or silicone baking mats.

Boil the milk and oil: Place the milk, oil, and salt in a medium saucepan and bring to a gentle boil over medium heat, stirring occasionally. Remove from heat as soon as you see big bubbles coming through the milk.

Add the tapioca flour: Add all of the tapioca flour and stir with a wooden spoon until you see no more dry tapioca flour. The dough will be grainy and gelatinous at this point.

Cool the dough: Transfer the dough to the bowl of a standing mixer fitted with a paddle attachment. (Alternatively, you can finish the dough by hand. Be prepared for a work-out.) Beat the dough for a few minutes at medium speed until it smooths out and has cooled enough that you can hold your finger against the dough for several seconds. There may be an oily slick that is not fully incorporated.

Beat in the eggs: With the mixer on medium speed, beat the eggs into the dough one at a time, waiting until the first egg is fully incorporated before adding the second. Scrape down the sides of the bowl as needed.

Beat in the cheese: Beat in the cheese on medium speed until fully incorporated. The resulting dough will be very sticky, stretchy, and soft with a consistency between cake batter and cookie dough. It will not be completely smooth.

Portion the puffs: Have a small bowl of water ready. For small puffs, scoop the dough by level tablespoons onto the baking sheets, spacing them about 1 1/2-inches apart (24 per baking sheet). For larger puffs, scoop the dough with a small (1 ounce or 2 tablespoon) ice cream scoop, spacing them about 2-inches apart (12 per baking sheet). Dip your scoop in water between scoops to prevent sticking.

Bake the puffs: Place the baking sheets in the oven and immediately reduce the heat to 350°F. Bake for 15 minutes. Rotate the baking sheets between racks and from front to back. Bake until the puffs have puffed, the outsides are dry, and they are just starting to turn golden-brown on the bottoms, 10 to 15 minutes more. (The tops will not brown much.) Cool for a few minutes and eat warm.

CORNBREAD-

Ingredients

For the Cornbread:

3 1/2 cups fine-ground cornmeal

1 3/4 cups all-purpose flour

2 1/2 teaspoons kosher salt

1 3/8 cups granulated sugar

2 1/4 cups whole milk

5 eggs, at room temperature

1 1/4 cups (2 1/2 sticks) unsalted butter, melted and cooled

For the Cornbread:

Preheat the oven to 425 (F) and prepare your pan by liberally spraying with cooking spray and lining with a piece of parchment paper; spray the parchment paper with cooking spray as well.

In a large bowl, combine 3 1/2 cups cornmeal, 1 3/4 cups flour, 1 3/4 tablespoons baking powder, and 2 1/2 teaspoons salt. Whisk until combined. Use a pint glass (or a bottle) to create a well in the center of the dry ingredients, and set aside.

In a large bowl, combine 1 3/8 cups granulated sugar, 2 1/4 cups whole milk, 5 eggs, and 1 1/4 cups melted butter. Whisk until thoroughly combined and the mixture is smooth — this'll take a surprisingly long amount of time because there is a LOT of the ingredients involved. Your arm will get tired, but persevere!

Once the mixture is smooth, pour the mixture into the well made by the dry ingredients (from the 2nd step). Use a rubber spatula to mix together, making sure to only mix until the ingredients are just combined. Again, this will take a long time because the batter is pretty thick and hearty, but you can do it!

Once the ingredients are well combined and the batter is an even, thick yellow, transfer to your baking pan and bake in the preheated oven for 35 minutes, or until a skewer inserted into the center of the bread comes out clean. If the top of the cornbread browns too quickly, cover with aluminum foil. Let rest on a wire rack for 10 to 15 minutes, before serving immediately.

FAVOURITE LEMON LOAF

Ingredients

½ cup butter or ½ cup margarine or ½ cup shortening (We prefer butter)

1 cup sugar

2 eggs

½ cup milk, 2% is fine

1 ½ cups all-purpose flour

1 teaspoon baking powder

½ teaspoon salt

1 lemon, rind of

Glaze

1 lemon, juice of

¼ cup sugar

Directions

In a large bowl, cream butter and sugar.

Add eggs, one at a time, beating until creamy.

Blend in milk.

In another bowl, mix together flour, baking powder, salt and lemon rind.

Pour into batter.

Stir to moisten.

Scrape into greased 9 x 5 inch loaf pan.

Bake in 350f degree oven for 55 to 60 minutes.

Cool in pan for 5 minutes.

Remove to rack and while still hot, with a toothpick poke holes all over the top of the loaf, and spoon glaze evenly over.

Cool.

Glaze: Combine lemon juice and sugar in saucepan.

Stir and heat till sugar is dissolved.

Spoon evenly over top of hot loaf.

HOLIDAY RUM EGGNOG BREAD

Ingredients

2 eggs

1 cup eggnog

2 teaspoons rum extract

2 1/4 cups all-purpose flour

1/4-1/2 cup walnuts, chopped

1/2 teaspoon salt

1 cup white sugar

1/2 cup butter, melted

1 teaspoon vanilla extract

2 teaspoons baking powder

1/4 teaspoon ground nutmeg

Directions

Preheat oven to 350°.

Grease only the bottom of a 9x5 loaf pan (or three 5 3/4 x 3 1/4 inch loaf pans). In a large bow beat the eggs.

Blend in sugar, eggnog, butter, rum extract and vanilla extract.

Combine the flour, baking powder, walnuts, salt and nutmeg, stirring to combine.

Mix into the eggnog mixture; stir just enough to moisten the dry ingredients.

Pour the batter into pan(s).

If baking bread in large pan, bake 40-60 minutes, or until a tester in the center comes out clean.

If baking the breads in the smaller pans, bake 35-40 minutes.

Cool 10 minutes, then remove from pan.

Cool breads completely, then wrap tightly. Keep in the refrigerator.

SPICED ANJOU PEAR BREAD

Ingredients

2 cups light brown sugar

1 cup vegetable oil

1⁄4 cup molasses

3 eggs

1 1⁄4 teaspoons salt

1 teaspoon baking soda

1 1⁄2 teaspoons ground cinnamon

1 1⁄2 teaspoons ground ginger

3⁄4 teaspoon ground cloves

1⁄4 teaspoon ground allspice

4 very firm d' Anjou pears, peeled, cored and thinly sliced

3 cups all-purpose flour

Directions

Preheat oven to 350F

Generously grease two large (9X5-inch) loaf pans--the long pieces of pear make the loaves more susceptible to sticking in the pans and falling apart, so make sure you grease generously.

In a large bowl, combine brown sugar, vegetable oil, molasses, and eggs; mix in salt, baking soda, cinnamon, ginger, cloves, and allspice.

Stir the pear slices in, coating them evenly; stir in the flour.

Pour batter into prepared loaf pans.

Bake for 50-65 minutes

Allow loaves to cool in pan about ten minutes before removing them and placing them on a wire rack to cool.

BANANA CHOCOLATE CHIP LOAF

Ingredients

2 cups all-purpose flour

1/4 cup granulated sugar

2 teaspoons baking powder

1 teaspoon baking soda

1 pinch salt

1 cup chocolate chips

2 cups bananas, 2-3 bananas, ripe, mashed

1/2 cup butter, melted

1/4 cup milk

2 eggs

Directions

Preheat oven to 350F.

In large bowl, whisk flour, sugar, baking powder, baking soda and salt ; add chocolate chips.

In separate bowl, whisk together bananas, butter, milk and eggs; pour over flour mixture and stir just until blended. Spread in greased 9- x 5-inch (2 L) loaf pan.

Bake in centre of oven at 350°F for 50 to 60 minutes or until cake tester inserted in centre comes out clean.

Let cool in pan on rack for 15 minutes. Turn out onto rack; let cool completely.

ALMOND CRANBERRY BREAD

Ingredients

2 cups flour

½ cup sugar

2 teaspoons baking powder

1 teaspoon salt

1 egg

¼ cup 1% low-fat milk

½ cup butter, melted

2 teaspoons almond extract

¼ cup almonds, chopped

1 ½ cups fresh cranberries (may use frozen ones too, just do not thaw before use)

1 tablespoon sugar (additional)

¼ cup almonds (slivered or sliced)

Directions

Preheat oven to 375F and grease a 8x4x2" loaf pan.

Combine the flour, sugar, baking powder, and salt in a medium bowl.

Combine the egg, milk, butter, and almond extract in a separate bowl.

Add the wet ingredients to the dry ingredients, mixing just until moistened (do not overmix).

Stir in chopped almonds and cranberries.

Spread batter in loaf pan and then sprinkle with additional 1 tbls. sugar and then the slivered or sliced almonds.

Bake for 30 minutes.

REDUCE heat to 350F and bake for an additional 20-30 minutes or until toothpick inserted in center comes out clean.

Let cool 10-15 minutes before removing from pan to wire rack.

EASY OLD FASHIONED ENGLISH STICKY GINGERBREAD LOAF

Ingredients

8 ounces self-rising flour

1 teaspoon baking powder

1 pinch salt

3 teaspoons ground ginger

2 ounces butter or 2 ounces margarine

2 ounces soft brown sugar

8 tablespoons black treacle

2 eggs, beaten and mixed with milk to make 1/2 pint

4 ounces raisins (optional)

Directions

Pre-heat oven to 180C/350F/Gas mark 4.

Grease and line a 2 lb loaf tin.

Mix the flour with the salt, baking powder, ground ginger & raisins if using.

Melt the butter or margarine and add the sugar, black treacle - mixing them together very well.

Add the butter mixture to the flour mixture - and mix with a wooden spoon.

Gradually beat in the egg and milk mixture to make a smooth, thick batter.

Pour into the greased and lined 2 lb loaf tin and bake for about 45 minutes, or until a skewer when inserted comes out clean.

The gingerbread loaf should be well risen and slightly sticky to the touch, although it gets stickier the longer it is kept.

Slice and eat warm with butter, or leave to go cold and store in an airtight container.

Also wonderful served warm with custard or cream.

BUTTERMILK CHOCOLATE BREAD

Ingredients

1 cup sugar

1⁄2 cup margarine or 1⁄2 cup butter, softened

2 eggs

1 cup buttermilk

1 3⁄4 cups all-purpose flour

1⁄2 cup unsweetened cocoa

1⁄2 teaspoon baking powder

1⁄2 teaspoon baking soda

1⁄2 teaspoon salt

1⁄3 cup chopped nuts

Directions

Heat oven to 350*.

Grease bottom only of 8x4 or 9x5-inch loaf pan.

In a large bowl, combine sugar and margarine; blend well.

Add eggs; blend well.

Stir in buttermilk.

Add flour, cocoa, baking powder, baking soda and salt; stir just until dry ingredients are moistened.

Stir in nuts.

Pour into greased pan.

Bake at 350* for 55 to 65 minutes or until toothpick inserted in center comes out clean.

Cool 15 minutes; remove from pan.

Cool completely.

PECAN MAPLE LOAF

Ingredients

1 1⁄2 cups all-purpose flour

1 teaspoon baking powder

3⁄4 cup butter

6 tablespoons sugar

1⁄2 cup pecans, roughly chopped

3 eggs

1 tablespoon milk

1 lemon, zest of

5 tablespoons maple syrup

Icing

6 tablespoons icing sugar (optional)

1 tablespoon lemon juice (optional)

2 tablespoons of roughly chopped pecans (optional)

Directions

Preheat oven, grease& line the base of a 9x5 loaf pan with baking/parchment paper.

Sift flour and baking powder into a bowl.

Cut butter into the flour and mix until the mixture looks like fine breadcrumbs.

Add in the sugar and pecans.

Beat eggs together with milk and lemon zest in a seperate bowl.

Stir in maple syrup.

Add this to the flour mixture and gently mix together.

Do not overmix, only until all dry ingredients have become moist.

The batter should be lumpy.

Pour batter into pan and smooth out the surface of the batter.

Bake in the oven for about 50-60 minutes or until cake is lightly browned.

To make sure, insert a toothpick into the center of the cake and if it comes out clean then the cake is ready.

Cool cake in pan for at least 10 minutes then turn out and let it cool on the rack.

(For Icing) Sift the icing sugar into a small bowl and stir in the lemon juice to create a smooth icing.

Drizzle over the loaf and then sprinkle the chopped pecans over the icing.

Wait until the icing is set then slice.

SOUR CREAM APPLE CARDAMOM QUICK BREAD

Ingredients

8 tablespoons butter, softened

1/2 cup vegetable oil

1 cup sugar

1/2 cup brown sugar

2 eggs

1 teaspoon vanilla extract

1/2 cup sour cream

1 1/2 teaspoons ground cardamom

1/2 teaspoon salt

1/2 teaspoon baking powder

1/2 teaspoon baking soda

2 1/2 cups flour

1 cup chopped walnuts

2 cups grated apples (such as gala or fuji)

Directions

Preheat oven to 350°F.

Butter and flour two 6- to 8-cup loaf pans and reserve.

In a mixer, cream together the butter, oil and sugars.

Add the eggs, vanilla and sour cream.

Sift together the cardamom, salt, baking powder, baking soda and flour.

Mix into the creamed ingredients, a little at a time, until incorporated, taking care not to overmix.

Stir in the walnuts and apple.

Divide batter between the prepared pans.

Tap pans on the counter to remove any air bubbles.

Bake for approximately 60 to 65 minutes, or until a toothpick poked in centers comes out clean.

Rotate pans halfway through baking.

After 45 minutes, place sheets of foil loosely over loaves to prevent overbrowning.

(Ovens bake differently, so use your best judgment and a doneness test when gauging cooking time for baked goods.) Cool in pans for 10 minutes, then remove to a rack and turn right-side-up to cool completely.

CINNAMON RAISIN BREAD FOR THE BREAD MACHINE

Ingredients

1 cup water

2 tablespoons margarine

3 cups flour

3 tablespoons sugar

1 1/2 teaspoons salt

1 teaspoon cinnamon

2 1/2 teaspoons yeast

3/4 cup raisins

Directions

Add all the ingredients in order given except the raisins.

Add raisins in on the "add in" beep.

Bake on "sweet bread" setting.

MOIST & DELICIOUS BANANA NUT BREAD

Ingredients

1⁄2 cup butter (or margarine)

1 1⁄4 cups sugar

1 teaspoon vanilla

2 eggs (beaten)

3 ripe bananas, smashed (about 1 cup)

1⁄4 cup milk

2 cups flour

1⁄2 teaspoon salt

1⁄2 teaspoon baking soda

1⁄2-1 cup chopped pecans (optional) or 1⁄2-1 cup walnuts (optional)

Directions

Cream butter & sugar. Add vanilla & eggs. Combine dry ingredients, add alternately with bananas & milk. Add nuts if desired. Grease & flour 1 bread pan (2-3 smaller pans) or pour into muffin cups. For loaf bake at 350 for 45-60 minute Muffins 350 for 20-25min. Enjoy!

CHRISTMAS STOLLEN

Ingredients

250 ml milk

50 g fresh yeast

70 g sugar

500 g all-purpose flour

3 egg yolks

180 g butter, melted cooled

2 tablespoons rum

250 g mixed dried fruit, small pieces (apricots,raisins,cherry,cranberry...)

100 g candied fruit (orange,lemon,cherry...)

½ teaspoon ground aniseed

¼ teaspoon ground nutmeg

100 g slivered almonds

1 orange, zest of

1 lemon, zest of

Directions

In a small bowl dissolve the yeast in the warm milk.

In a large bowl put sugar, flour, egg yolks, butter rum add yeast mixture and using a wooden spoon stir all ingredients together.

Turn dough out onto a lightly floured surface and knead by hands until comes together than add dry fruit (chopped into small pieces), candied fruit, anise, nutmeg, almonds and zests.

Knead until you have moderately stiff and smooth dough. About 8-10 minutes.

Shape into a ball. Place into greased bowl, turning once to grease surface. Cover with plastic wrap.

Let it rise in a warm place until double in size about 1 1/2 hours.

After that punch dough down. Turn out onto a lightly floured surface.

Roll out into rectangle 4cm thick and then fold the long side over by half and other side over the first half (like business letter).

Carefully transfer the dough to the baking sheet. Let it rest for 20 minutes covered with towel.

Preheat oven to 180°C

Bake until golden brown about 30-40 minutes or until a wooden toothpick comes out clean.

While still hot brush with melted butter and sift a lot of icing sugar over the top.

CRANBERRY SWIRL LOAF

Ingredients

Bread

3 -3 1⁄2 cups flour

1⁄3 cup sugar

1 (1/4 ounce) package fast rise yeast

1⁄2 teaspoon salt

1⁄2 cup water

1⁄2 cup milk

1⁄3 cup butter, cubed

Filling

1 cup fresh cranberries or 1 cup frozen cranberries

1⁄4 cup brown sugar

1⁄4 cup water

1 tablespoon butter, cubed

1⁄2 cup walnuts, chopped

1 tablespoon lemon juice

Topping

2 tablespoons flour

2 tablespoons sugar

2 tablespoons butter, cold and divided

Directions

In large mixing bowl, combine 1 cup flour, sugar, yeast and salt. In saucepan, heat water, milk, and butter to 120-130 (I did this in the microwave). Add to dry ingredients, beat until combined. Stir in enough remaining flour to form a soft dough.

Turn onto a floured surface, knead until smooth and elastic, about 5-7 minutes. Place in a greased bowl, turning once to grease top. Cover and let rise in a warm place until doubled, about 1 hour.

For filling, combine cranberries, brown sugar, and water in small saucepan. Cook over medium heat until berries pop, about 15 minutes. Remove from heat, stir in butter, walnuts, and lemon juice. Cool.

Punch dough down. Turn onto a lightly floured surface; roll into a 20-in. x 10-in. rectangle. Spread cooled filling to within 1/2 inches of edges. Roll up jelly-roll style, starting with a long side; pinch seam to seal. Place in a zigzag pattern in a greased 9-in. x 5-in. x 3-in. loaf pan.

For topping, combine flour and sugar in a small bowl; cut in 1 tablespoon butter until crumbly. Melt remaining butter; brush over dough. Sprinkle with topping. Cover and let rise until doubled, about 40 minutes. Bake at 350° for 40-45 minutes or until bread sounds hollow when tapped. Cool in pan for 10 minutes then carefully remove from pan to a wire rack to cool.

SPICED APPLE LOAF

Ingredients

9 ounces plain flour

6 ounces caster sugar

5 ounces soft butter or 5 ounces margarine

3 ounces sultanas

1 egg

1 teaspoon ground nutmeg

1 teaspoon ground mixed spice

1 -2 teaspoon ground cinnamon

1 teaspoon baking powder

2 -3 bramley cooking apples

Directions

Pre-heat oven to gas 4 or 180.

Line a 2lb loaf tin with greasproof paper.

Peel and core the apples, cut into chunks, place in a pan and cover with water, bring to the boil and simmer until the apples are just starting to soften. Drain and add a little sugar to taste (I prefer the apples to be quite tart). Leave to one side to cool.

Put all dry ingredients into a large bowl together and mix roughly.

Next add all wet ingredients at same time, mix until all of the flour mixture is taken up.

Pour into the loaf tin and cook for 1 1/4 - 1 1/2 hours until browned.

When the cake is cooked, LEAVE IT IN THE TIN until cool, then wrap in foil.

This cake is best left until the next day to eat (if you can wait that long!).

BANANA BREAD FRENCH TOAST

INGREDIENTS

4 large eggs

1/4 c. whole milk

1 tsp. pure vanilla extract

1 tsp. ground cinnamon

pinch of kosher salt

2 tbsp. butter

Leftover banana bread (this recipe uses 3/4 loaf)

Sliced banana, for serving

Chocolate chips, for serving

Maple syrup, for serving

DIRECTIONS

In a medium bowl, whisk together eggs, milk, vanilla, cinnamon, and salt.

In a large skillet over medium heat, melt butter. Working in batches, coat banana bread with egg mixture for 30 seconds, then place in heated skillet.

Cook until golden, 2 to 3 minutes per side. Top with sliced bananas and chocolate chips, and drizzle with maple syrup.

CARROT CAKE BANANA BREAD

INGREDIENTS

FOR THE BANANA BREAD

Cooking spray, for pan

1/2 c. melted butter

3/4 c. sugar

1/2 c. brown sugar

2 large eggs

1/4 c. whole milk

1 tsp. pure vanilla extract

2 c. all-purpose flour

1 tsp. baking powder

1/2 tsp. baking soda

1 tsp. ground cinnamon

1/4 tsp. kosher salt

1/4 tsp. ground nutmeg

3 large ripe bananas, mashed

1/4 c. grated carrots

1/4 c. chopped pecans, plus more for garnish

FOR THE CREAM CHEESE FROSTING

8 oz. block cream cheese, softened

1 c. butter, softened

1 tsp. pure vanilla extract

1/4 tsp. kosher salt

1/2 c. powdered sugar

DIRECTIONS

Preheat oven to 350°, then grease a 9"-x-5" loaf pan with cooking spray and line it with parchment paper.

In a large bowl, stir together butter and sugars until combined. Add eggs, milk and vanilla and mix until combined. Slowly add in flour, baking powder, baking soda, cinnamon, salt and nutmeg and stir until completely incorporated. Gently fold in mashed bananas, grated carrots and pecans and mix until fully combined.

Pour batter into prepared pan and smooth top with a spatula. Bake until a toothpick has moist crumbs, about 1 hour, then let cool.

Make frosting: In a large bowl using a hand mixer, beat cream cheese and butter until smooth. Beat in vanilla, salt and powdered sugar until fluffy.

Once cool, frost bread and garnish with pecans.

STRAWBERRY SHORTCAKE BANANA BREAD

INGREDIENTS

1 c. butter, 1/2 cup melted and 1/2 cup softened, plus more for buttering pan

1 1/2 c. all-purpose flour, plus for flouring pan

1 tsp. baking soda

1/4 tsp. kosher salt

1 c. sugar

1/4 c. buttermilk

1 tsp. vanilla extract

1 egg plus 1 egg yolk

1 c. sliced strawberries, plus more for serving

3 super ripe bananas, mashed

Freshly whipped cream, for serving

DIRECTIONS

Preheat oven to 350 degrees F and butter and flour a 9-x-5" loaf pan.

In a large bowl, whisk together 1 cup flour, baking soda, and salt.

In another large bowl, combine 3/4 cup sugar, 1/2 cup butter, buttermilk, vanilla, egg and egg yolk until smooth. Pour wet ingredients over dry and stir until combined, then fold in strawberries and mashed bananas.

Make crumb topping: Combine remaining 1/2 cup flour, remaining 1/4 cup sugar, remaining 1/2 cup butter, and a pinch of salt.

Transfer batter to prepared baking dish and top with crumb topping. Bake until deeply golden and a toothpick comes out clean, about 60 minutes. Let cool at least 10 minutes before serving.

To serve as a shortcake, stack banana bread with freshly whipped cream and strawberries.

BROWN BUTTER SODA BREAD

INGREDIENTS:

Soda Bread:

1/4 cup (1/2 stick) unsalted butter

2 cups all purpose flour

1 1/2 cups whole wheat flour

1/2 cup oats

1 tablespoon packed brown sugar

2 teaspoons baking powder

1 teaspoon baking soda

1 teaspoon salt

1 3/4 cups buttermilk

1/2 cup dried currants

1 egg white, beaten

Honey- Butter (optional):

1/2 cup unsalted butter, softened

1 tablespoon honey

1 or 2 shakes of ground cinnamon

DIRECTIONS:

1. Preheat the oven to 375°F.

2. Melt the butter in small saucepan over medium heat until melted and golden brown (stirring often and keeping a close

eye), 3 to 4 minutes. Remove the pan from heat and set it aside to cool.

3. In a large bowl, whisk together the flours, oats, brown sugar, baking powder, baking soda and salt. Stir in the brown butter and buttermilk until the flour mixture is moistened and comes together.

4. Turn the dough out onto a well-floured work surface. Sprinkle the currants on top and knead them gently into the dough until the dough comes together, about 7 turns. Divide the dough in half. Shape each half into ball, and lightly flatten each into 6-inch round. Place the rounds on ungreased baking sheet, spacing 5 inches apart. Use a knife to cut a 1/2-inch deep "X" in the top of each round of dough. Brush the tops with the egg wash.

5. Bake the loaves until they turn deep golden brown and tester inserted into center comes out clean, about 40 to 45 minutes. Cool breads on rack at least 10 minutes. Serve warm or at room temperature.

6. If you'd like to make the honey butter, just mix the butter with honey and cinnamon in a small bowl until blended. Serve with the bread.

APRICOT ORANGE IRISH SODA BREAD

Ingredients

2 cups all purpose flour, plus 1 tablespoon to toss with the dried apricots

2 cups whole wheat white flour*

2 tablespoons granulated sugar

1 teaspoon baking soda

1½ teaspoons salt

4 tablespoons cold unsalted butter, cut into ½" dice

1¾ cup cold low fat buttermilk, shaken

1 egg

zest of 1 medium orange

1 cup chopped dried apricots

Instructions

Preheat oven to 375 degrees. Line a baking sheet with parchment paper.

Add the dry ingredients to the bowl of a stand mixer fitted with the paddle attachment, or use your handheld electric mixer. Mix the dry ingredients on low speed.

Add the cold butter cubes and mix on low speed until the butter is completely mixed into the dry ingredients. Use your fingers if necessary to work any large chunks of butter into the flour.

Using a fork, beat the egg, buttermilk, and zest in a measuring cup. Turn the mixer on low speed, and slowly add the wet ingredients to the dry ingredients, mixing just until combined.

Toss the dried apricots with the reserved tablespoon of flour, then mix into the dough on low speed just until combined. The dough will be VERY wet!

Pour the dough out onto a well floured surface and sprinkle with flour. Flour your hands, and knead a few times until it's in the shape of a round loaf. Place on the prepared baking sheet. Using a serrated knife, cut a small "X" into the center.

Bake 45-55 minutes or until a cake tester comes out clean. Cool on a wire rack.

BREAKFAST IRISH SODA BREAD W/ DRIED CHERRIES & GOLDEN RAISINS

INGREDIENTS:

3 cups all-purpose flour

1/4 cup light brown sugar, packed

3 teaspoons baking powder

1 teaspoon baking soda

1 teaspoon salt

4 Tablespoons cold, unsalted butter, cut into pieces

1 1/4 cups buttermilk

1 large egg

1 large egg yolk

3/4 cup golden raisins

3/4 cup dried cherries

plus a few more raisins and cherries

extra flour for dusting & kneading

DIRECTIONS:

1. Position a rack in the middle of the oven. Preheat oven to 400 degrees F. Line a baking sheet with parchment paper.

2. In the bowl of a food processor, combine flour, sugar, baking powder, baking soda and salt. Give it a couple of pulses, then add the butter pieces; pulse until butter is incorporated and small crumbs are formed.

3. Pour flour/butter mixture into a large bowl and make a well in the center. Add buttermilk, egg, and egg yolk and stir just until moistened. Then stir in the 3/4 cup raisins and 3/4 cup cherries.

4. Turn the dough out onto a lightly floured surface and knead gently 5 to 10 times (dusting flour lightly onto dough if it's too sticky). Knead just until the dough comes together and is smooth. Divide dough in half and shape each half into a round. Stud a few extra raisins and cherries into the tops of the loaves. Dust the tops of the rounds lightly with a little flour.

5. Transfer rounds to prepared baking sheet, leaving about three inches between them. Place another baking sheet of the same size underneath to prevent burning. With a sharp knife, slash the tops with a large X about 1/2-inch deep.

6. Bake until dark brown and crusty, 35 to 40 minutes, or until toothpick inserted into the center of the X comes out clean. The loaf will sound hollow when tapped on the side.

7. Serve warm or at room temperature. Store wrapped in plastic at room temperature or freeze in a zip bag for up to 2 months.

CINNAMON RAISIN IRISH SODA BREAD

Ingredients:

5 cups flour

1 cup sugar

4 teaspoon baking powder

2 teaspoons McCormick Caraway Seeds

1 teaspoon McCormick Ground Cinnamon

1/2 teaspoon baking soda

1/2 teaspoon salt

3/4 cups raisins or currants

3 eggs

1 cup buttermilk

1 cup sour cream

1 teaspoon McCormick Pure Vanilla Extract

Directions:

Preparation: Heat oven to 350 degrees F. Lightly grease baking sheet.

Place flour, sugar, baking powder, caraway seed, cinnamon, baking soda and salt in a bowl and mix to combine. Stir in raisins. Set aside. Beat eggs in a bowl. Stir in buttermilk, sour cream and vanilla, then add to dry ingredients and stir until well combined.

Divide dough in half. Shape each portion into a ball. Place on prepared baking sheet. Make a deep X on top of each loaf with a knife. Bake at 350 degrees for about 50-55 minutes or until toothpick inserted in the center comes out clean and top is golden brown. Transfer loaves to a wire rack to cool.

BROWN BUTTER SODA BREAD

INGREDIENTS:

Soda Bread:

1/4 cup (1/2 stick) unsalted butter

2 cups all purpose flour

1 1/2 cups whole wheat flour

1/2 cup oats

1 tablespoon packed brown sugar

2 teaspoons baking powder

1 teaspoon baking soda

1 teaspoon salt

1 3/4 cups buttermilk

1/2 cup dried currants

1 egg white, beaten

Honey- Butter (optional):

1/2 cup unsalted butter, softened

1 tablespoon honey

1 or 2 shakes of ground cinnamon

DIRECTIONS:

1. Preheat the oven to 375°F.

2. Melt the butter in small saucepan over medium heat until melted and golden brown (stirring often and keeping a close

eye), 3 to 4 minutes. Remove the pan from heat and set it aside to cool.

3. In a large bowl, whisk together the flours, oats, brown sugar, baking powder, baking soda and salt. Stir in the brown butter and buttermilk until the flour mixture is moistened and comes together.

4. Turn the dough out onto a well-floured work surface. Sprinkle the currants on top and knead them gently into the dough until the dough comes together, about 7 turns. Divide the dough in half. Shape each half into ball, and lightly flatten each into 6-inch round. Place the rounds on ungreased baking sheet, spacing 5 inches apart. Use a knife to cut a 1/2-inch deep "X" in the top of each round of dough. Brush the tops with the egg wash.

5. Bake the loaves until they turn deep golden brown and tester inserted into center comes out clean, about 40 to 45 minutes. Cool breads on rack at least 10 minutes. Serve warm or at room temperature.

6. If you'd like to make the honey butter, just mix the butter with honey and cinnamon in a small bowl until blended. Serve with the bread.

5-MINUTE ARTISAN BREAD RECIPE

INGREDIENTS

3 cups (24 ounces or 680 grams) lukewarm water (100°F or 38°C), plus more for the broiler tray

1 tablespoon (.35 ounce or 10 grams) granulated yeast (active dry, instant, quick rise, or bread machine is fine)

1 to 1 1/2 tablespoons (.6 to .9 ounce or 9 to 12 grams) kosher or other coarse salt, to taste

6 1/2 cups (2 pounds or 910 grams) unbleached all-purpose flour, measured by the scoop-and-sweep method

Cornmeal, for dusting (optional)

DIRECTIONS

1. Warm the 3 cups water just a little so that it feels just slightly warmer than body temperature. That should put it at about 100°F (40°C). In the large bowl of a standing mixer or a 6-quart container with a lid, mix the yeast, warm water, and salt. Don't worry about getting the yeast to dissolve. Add the flour all at once, then use a spoon or stand mixer to mix until the flour is completely incorporated and you have a blobby dough. (If you're hand-mixing the dough and it becomes too difficult to incorporate all the flour with the spoon, just use very wet hands to press the mixture together.) Don't knead the dough! It's not necessary. You just want the dough to be uniformly wet and loose enough to conform to the shape of its container. All you need to do is be certain that there are no dry patches of flour.

2. Loosely cover the container and let the dough hang out at room temperature until it begins to rise and collapse or at least flatten a little on the top, about 2 hours. (Relax. It's bread dough, not a newborn. You don't need to monitor it constantly. And don't worry about the dough being precisely double or

triple its original volume as you would with a traditional bread recipe. Just walk away, go about your business, and come back in 2 hours. Seriously.)

3. After 2 hours, stash the container of dough in the fridge. That's it. (If your container isn't vented, you want to ensure the gases can escape by leaving the cover open a crack for the first couple days in the fridge; after that, you can seal it.) You can use the dough anytime after the initial 2-hour rise, although the refrigerated wet dough is less sticky and easier to work with than dough at room temperature, so it's best to refrigerate the dough overnight before handling it. Once refrigerated, the dough will seem to have shrunk back upon itself as though it will never rise again—that's normal. Whatever you do, do not punch down this dough. You're trying to retain as much gas in the dough as possible, and punching it down knocks gas out and results in denser loaves. Just be certain to use the dough at some point within 14 days.

4. When you want to bake a loaf of artisan bread, dust a pizza peel or a baking sheet turned upside down with cornmeal or line it with parchment paper. Grab a hunk of the dough and use a serrated knife or scissors to cut off a 1-pound piece of dough. Hold the dough in your hands and, if necessary, add just enough flour so the dough doesn't stick to your hands. (What you're trying to do is surround the surface of the dough with flour so that it can be handled. You are not trying to incorporate more flour into the dough, so for the love of all things good, resist the temptation to get rid of all the dough's inherent and lovely stickiness by working the flour into the dough.) Gently stretch the surface of the dough, tucking the ends underneath the ball and rotating it a quarter turn as you go. Most of the dusting flour will fall off, and that's okay, because as we just said, it's not intended to be incorporated into the dough. The bottom of the ball of dough may appear to be a collection of bunched ends, but it will flatten out and adhere during resting and baking. Your round loaf of bread should be smooth and cohesive, and the

entire shaping process should take no more than 20 to 40 seconds—don't work the dough any longer or your loaves may be dense. Place the shaped ball of dough on the prepared pizza peel and let it rest for about 40 minutes. It doesn't need to be covered. You may not see much rise during this period, but don't fret. It will rise much more during baking.

5. Preheat the oven to 450°F (230°C) for at least 20 to 30 minutes. Preheat a baking stone on a middle rack for at least 20 to 30 minutes. Place an empty metal broiler tray on any rack that won't interfere with the rising bread. (Do not use a glass pan as it could shatter.)

6. Dust the top of the raised loaf generously with flour and, using a serrated bread knife, slash a 1/2-inch-deep cross or tic-tac-toe pattern in the top. There's no need to dust the flour off the loaf.

7. Place the far edge of the peel or the upside-down baking sheet in the oven on the baking stone a few inches beyond where you want the bread to land. Give the peel or baking sheet a couple quick back-and-forth jiggles and then abruptly pull it out from under the loaf. The loaf should land on the baking stone with very little drama. Quickly but carefully pour about 1 cup hot water into the broiler tray and immediately shut the oven door to trap the steam. Bake the bread for a total of 20 to 35 minutes, until the crust is richly browned and firm to the touch. (Don't worry. Because the dough is so wet, there's very little risk of it becoming dry despite how dark the crust may become.) And crazily enough, a perfectly baked loaf will audibly crackle, or "sing," when initially exposed to room temperature. Let the loaf cool completely, preferably on a wire rack for the best flavor, texture, and slicing. The crust may initially soften but will firm when cooled.

CARAWAY SEED BREAD RECIPE

ingredients

For the sourdough starter

100g dark rye flour

50g wholewheat flour

150g water

30g rye sourdough starter

For the main dough

180g strong white bread flour

80g dark rye flour

150g water

8g salt

10g caraway seeds

How to make caraway bread

Prepare the sourdough by combining the various ingredients in a medium bowl. Mix well and cover the bowl. Leave to rest overnight (16 – 24 hours).

On day 2, prepare the main dough by combining 300g of the sourdough from day 1 (the remaining 30g go back into the fridge for future bakes) with the main dough ingredients.

Mix well and knead the dough for at least 10 minutes.

Rest for about an hour, then shape into a loaf before placing it in your pre-floured proofing basket.

Leave to proof for a few hours (this will depend on your room temperature), then preheat the oven. If you have a La Cloche baking dome, preheat this in the oven from cold.

Turn out the loaf from your proofing basket to the baking tray (lined with baking paper) or the La Cloche dome.

Make a few slashes with your scoring knife.

Bake for 10 minutes at 220°C and for another 45 minutes at 200°C. Take the lid off the dome for the last 10 minutes if using the La Cloche dome.

Cool on a wire rack.

GRÜNKERN BREAD

Ingredients

For the sourdough

25g spelt sourdough starter

220g wholemeal spelt flour

220g water

For the Grünkern soaker

175g Grünkern

350g water

For the main dough

220g spelt flour

50g water

14g salt

1 tbsp malt extract

How to bake Grünkern bread

Day 1

Prepare the sourdough by combining your spelt starter with the spelt flour and water. Mix well in a bowl, cover with a lid and leave to stand at room temperature for 16 – 24 hours.

Combine Grünkern and water in a pan, cover and leave to soak overnight.

Day 2

Drain the Grünkern and bring to a boil in a pan with 350g water. Simmer over a low heat for about 15 minutes. Drain any remaining water.

In a large bowl, combine 440g of the sourdough (the remaining 25g go back into the fridge for your next bake) with the main dough ingredients.

Form a dough and knead for 10 minutes.

Add the Grünkern to the dough and knead until evenly distributed.

Place the dough back into the bowl, cover and leave to rest for 1 hour at room temperature.

Prepare a baking tin (23 x 11 x 9.5 cm) by lightly oiling it. I use a silicone brush to do that.

Place the dough into the tin and prove for 2 – 4 hours depending on the temperature in your room. The dough should rise visibly, filling the tin to the top.

Preheat the oven to 250°C.

Place the baking tin on the second layer from bottom up and bake for 15 minutes, then bake for a further 25 minutes at 180°C and a final 10 minutes outside the tin at 180°C.

Cool on a wire rack.

Made in the USA
Las Vegas, NV
29 October 2022